Bull Run to Atlanta:
The Civil War Letters of
Harry Comer
Company A, 1ˢᵗ Ohio Volunteer Infantry

Bull Run to Atlanta:
The Civil War Letters of Harry Comer
Company A, 1ˢᵗ Ohio Volunteer Infantry

Edited by Daniel A. Masters

Columbian Arsenal Press
Perrysburg, Ohio

Copyright © 2017 by Daniel A. Masters

All rights reserved. This book or any portion thereof may not be reproduced or used in any manner whatsoever without the express written permission of the publisher except for the use of brief quotations in a book review or scholarly journal.

First Printing: 2017

Library of Congress Cataloguing-in-Publication Data
Comer, Henry Harrison, 1836-1881.
Bull Run to Atlanta: The Civil War Letters of Harry Comer, Company A, 1st Ohio Volunteer Infantry/edited by Daniel A. Masters
p.   cm.
ISBN: 978-1-365-68140-0
1. Comer, Henry Harrison, 1836-1881. 2. Soldiers-United States-Biography. 3. United States Army-Biography 4. United States History-Civil War, 1861-1865-Personal narratives   5. United States History-Civil War, 1861-1865-Campaigns
I. Masters, Daniel A.   II. Title
973.7092

Columbian Arsenal Press
1310 Mary Lou Ct.
Perrysburg, Ohio 43551
Email: Dam1941@aol.com

For Sam,
With a father's love in hopes to perpetuate the study of this, our Civil War, and to preserve the memory of the brave men who wore the blue from 1861-65.

Contents

Introduction

Chapter One: Ninety Days to Bull Run Pgs. 9-27

1. Harrisburg Encampment, Pennsylvania, April 21, 1861
2. Lancaster, Pennsylvania, April 27, 1861
3. Camp McClelland, near Philadelphia, Pennsylvania, May 8, 1861
4. Washington, D.C., May 27, 1861
5. Camp Sherman, Washington, D.C., June 1, 1861
6. Pine Hill Camp, Fairfax Co., Virginia, June 16, 1861
7. Camp Upton, Fairfax Co., Virginia, July 11, 1861
8. Washington, D.C., July 24, 1861

Chapter Two: A Winter in Kentucky, 1861-1862 Pgs. 28-52

9. Camp Corwin, Dayton, Ohio, August 29, 1861
10. Camp Corwin, Dayton, Ohio, September 8, 1861
11. Camp Corwin, Dayton, Ohio, September 21, 1861
12. Camp Corwin, Dayton, Ohio, October 16, 1861
13. Camp Yoke near Nashville Depot, Louisville, Kentucky, November 8, 1861
14. Camp Armstrong, Hardin Co., Kentucky, November 14, 1861
15. Camp Nevin, Hardin Co., Kentucky, November 21, 1861
16. Camp Nevin, Hardin Co., Kentucky, November 26, 1861
17. Camp en route, Kentucky, December 10, 1861
18. Camp Wood, Green River, Hart Co., Kentucky, December 22, 1861
19. Camp Wood, Green River, Hart Co., Kentucky, December 29, 1861
20. Camp Wood, Green River, Hart Co., Kentucky, January 1, 1862
21. Camp Wood, Green River, Hart Co., Kentucky, January 12, 1862
22. Camp Wood, Green River, Hart Co., Kentucky, January 18, 1862
23. Camp Wood, Green River, Hart Co., Kentucky, January 31, 1862

Chapter Three: Shiloh, Corinth, and the summer of 1862 Pgs. 53-72

24. Camp Andy Johnson, near Nashville, Tennessee, March 12, 1862
25. Camp in the woods near Pittsburg Landing, Tennessee, April 16, 1862
26. Field of Shiloh near Pittsburg Landing, Tennessee, April 25, 1862
27. Camp near Corinth, Mississippi, May 27, 1862
28. Indian Creek, Limestone Co., Alabama, late June 1862
29. Cowan Station, Franklin Co., Tennessee, July 9, 1862

Chapter Four: Stones River and Murfreesboro Pgs. 73-87

30. Camp near Nashville, Tennessee, December 1, 1862
31. Camp four miles from Murfreesboro, Tennessee, January 8, 1863
32. Camp near Murfreesboro, Tennessee, February 1, 1863
33. Camp Drake, Murfreesboro, Tennessee, March 23, 1863
34. Camp Drake, Murfreesboro, Tennessee, April 6, 1863

Chapter Five: Onward to Chattanooga Pgs. 88-116

35. Camp Drake, Murfreesboro, Tennessee, June 5, 1863
36. Steamer Glide, off Fort Donelson, Tennessee, August 3, 1863
37. Tullahoma Guardhouse, Tullahoma, Tennessee, August 15, 1863
38. Weed Patch No. 3287, Alabama, September 1-8, 1863
39. Chattanooga, Tennessee, September 27, 1863
40. Missionary Ridge, Chattanooga, Tennessee, November 27, 1863

Chapter Six: Eastern Tennessee to Atlanta Pgs. 117-123

41. Near Knoxville, Tennessee, December 14, 1863
42. Knoxville, Tennessee, April 4, 1864
43. Kingston, Cass Co., Georgia, June 5, 1864
44. Chattanooga, Tennessee, August 21, 1864

Rosters of Company A, 1st Ohio Volunteer Infantry Pgs. 124-129

Rosters of Company A, 1st Ohio Volunteer Infantry Pgs. 124-129

Battle Narrative and Service of the 1st O.V.I. Pgs. 130-139

Index

Endotes

Illustrations

1. Pen and ink drawing of Private Harry Comer, pg. 8 (Abby Kitcher)

2. Maj. Gen. Alexander McDowell McCook, pg. 20 (Library of Congress)

3. Map of the First Battle of Bull Run, July 21, 1861 pg. 23 (Hal Jespersen)

4. Col. Alexander M. McCook and Lt. Col. Edwin A. Parrott, 1st Ohio Volunteer Infantry, pg. 35 (Larry M. Strayer Collection)

5. Pen and ink drawing of Jake Starling and Jim Collier, sutlers, pg. 41 (Abby Kitcher)

6. Brig. Gen. Lovell Harrison Rousseau, pg. 57 (Library of Congress)

7. Map of the Battle of Shiloh, April 7, 1862 pg. 62 (Hal Jespersen)

8. Engraving of the 1st Ohio Infantry at the Battle of Shiloh, pg. 72 (Leslie's Illustrated Newspaper)

9. Maj. Gen. William Starke Rosecrans, pg. 75 (Library of Congress)

10. Union infantry on the retreat at Stones River, pg. 77 (Battles and Leaders)

11. Map of the Battle of Stones River, December 31, 1862, pg. 78 (David T. Dixon/Hal Jespersen)

12. Capt. Henry Dornbush, Company E, pg. 85 (Larry M. Strayer Collection)

13. Pen and ink drawing of Comer languishing in the guardhouse, pg. 94 (Abby Kitcher)

14. Major Joab Arwin Stafford, 1st Ohio Volunteer Infantry, pg. 98 (Generals in Blue)

15. Confederate infantry at the Battle of Chickamauga, pg. 100 (Battles and Leaders)

16. Map of the Battle of Chickamauga, September 19, 1863, pg. 101 (Hal Jespersen)

17. Map of the Battle of Chickamauga, September 20, 1863, pg. 102 (Hal Jespersen)

18. Lt. Col. Elisha B. Langdon, 1st Ohio Volunteer Infantry, pg. 108 (Larry M. Strayer Collection)

19. Battle of Missionary Ridge, November 25, 1863, pg. 112 (Hal Jespersen)

20. Missionary Ridge in 1863 pg. 113 (Library of Congress)

21. Map of the Atlanta Campaign, May-July 1864, pg. 121 (Hal Jespersen)

Acknowledgements

I would like to thank the following friends and associates who helped bring this project to life: Robert Van Dorn of Findlay, Ohio, Larry M. Strayer of Urbana, Ohio, Rob Tong of Findlay, Ohio, Richard Baranowski of Way Public Library in Perrysburg, Ohio, Donna Christian of the Local History Department of the Toledo-Lucas County Public Library, author David T. Dixon who graciously permitted the republication of the Stones River battlefield map that he commissioned for his stellar work on Charles Anderson of the 93rd Ohio, cartographer Hal Jespersen whose superb map work illustrates this volume, Perrysburg High School art teacher Lynn Barefoot, and her gifted student Abby Kitcher who rendered several drawings for this work.

My deepest thanks go to my beloved wife Amy who has provided constant support, encouragement, and infinite patience during the many hours spent pursuing this passion for Civil War history.

Introduction

The 44 letters contained in this volume from the able pen of Private Henry Harrison "Harry" Comer of Company A, 1st Ohio Volunteer Infantry provide a fascinating glimpse into the life of a regular soldier in the Army of the Cumberland. Comer penned these letters specifically for publication in the newspaper that once employed him as a "typo," the *Weekly Lancaster Gazette* later renamed *The Lancaster Gazette*. The letters begin shortly after his enlistment in the spring of 1861 and follow the 1st Ohio throughout its three years' Civil War service in the Eastern and Western theaters.

The *first* 1st Ohio Volunteer Infantry regiment mustered into service in April 1861 in response to President Lincoln's call for 75,000 volunteers to put down the Rebellion in the wake of the fall of Fort Sumter. Comer was among the first to enlist, and the first eight letters of this collection follow the ninety day regiment through its travels from Ohio to Pennsylvania to the outskirts of Washington, D.C., where his regiment took its place with the Army of the Northeastern Virginia (precursor to the Army of the Potomac) and fought at the first battle of Bull Run.

Upon the completion of its ninety day service, the regiment returned to Ohio where it recruited and again took the field for three years' service, with Comer again documenting all the news from Company A. Assigned to the western theater forces in Kentucky, the 1st Ohio served for much of its existence under General Alexander McDowell McCook, the regiment's colonel during its ninety day service who later served as a brigade, division, and eventually corps commander in the Army of the Cumberland. The 1st Ohio took part in the spring 1862 invasion of Tennessee, fought at the battles of Shiloh, Stones River, Chickamauga, and Missionary Ridge before being sent to Knoxville at the end of 1863. The regiment spent the winter there before embarking on Sherman's drive to Atlanta in May 1864.

Comer's letters document not just the movements of his regiment and the comings and goings of the men in his company, but also provide insight into how the war changed the men who fought it. As an example, the tone of Comer's letters show a marked shift: from the 'boy adventurer' of 1861 out to see the world with eyes wide open, giddily pointing out the sights and sounds of faraway places to his hometown readers, to the hard cynical veteran in 1864 who excoriated the denizens of Knoxville as constituting "one of the most God-forsaken, law-defying, conglomerated masses of vice and immorality that Heaven in its mercy ever permitted to exist." Comer didn't shy away from the seedier side of life, describing for his readers the corrosive effect of the war's privations on the civilian population, in both their material and moral aspects.

His letters do not often dwell on grand strategy or political matters; we never learn of Comer's opinion of the Emancipation Proclamation, for instance, but it is clear that he harbored an intense dislike for Copperheads ("Vallandighammers" in Comer's parlance) and his support for an undivided Union remained strong throughout the war. Comer viewed his Confederate opponents with a jaundiced eye; he respected their courage in battle, but took pains to dismissively refer to them as the "chivalry" and often commented on the raggedness of the Confederate army, an army he, early in the war, described as a "horde of political blacklegs, bankrupt politicians, refugees from foreign climes and crimes, murderers, thieves, pick pockets and assassins." His opinion softened somewhat over the course of the war, later referring to the Confederate Army as merely the "grease-encased hordes of Rebeldom."

Sociable, puckish, and not above embellishment, Comer's observations of his comrades and their foibles provide some levity in what could otherwise be a tedious batch of correspondence documenting marches and the boredom of camp life. Comer is perhaps at his best in describing those around him: from escaped slaves to army sutlers, "bogus" refugees to army shirks, pretentious officers and even regular "high privates in the rear rank" such as himself. Comer viewed the world with an eye towards the absurd and life in the Army of the Cumberland provided ample fodder for Comer's pen.

But life in the army was no lark, and the experience wore thin after years of exposure to the hardships and privations of field service. By the summer of 1863, Comer was counting the days left on his enlistment and significantly, he (and the majority of his regiment for that matter) chose not to re-enlist for the balance of the war in early 1864. After the sanguinary battle of Mission Ridge, Comer wrote wearily "God grant we may have no more Missionary Ridges to capture but many more as brilliant victories." He took sick not long after the start of the Atlanta campaign in May 1864 (Comer described the ailment as heart palpitations brought on by violent nervous excitement), and spent the remainder of his service observing the war from a hospital.

The regulations, drill and monotony of life in camp did not sit well with the free-wheeling Comer, who often commented acidly on official "red tape" and the officious commissioned officers as "red tapists." Comer had a mixed relationship with his company officers: while he was effusive in praise for his original company commander Captain Joab Arwin Stafford, he seemed to enjoy a less chummy relationship with Stafford's replacement Emanuel T. Hooker, who delighted in placing Comer on extra duty. "Hooker and I can't agree, I don't see why," Comer once lamented. In October 1862, Hooker had Comer reduced to the ranks for "neglect of duty" and by May 1863, transferred him out of Company A altogether.

As a soldier, Comer ultimately made little pretense of being exceptional, especially after the first flush of enthusiasm of being in the army wore off. He made no claims of being brave or steadfast in action; his accounts of battles document the heroic actions of others, presumably with Comer as the quiet scribe nearby taking it all in. Early in the war, he fancied himself a "model soldier," but as time progressed, Comer evidenced a more self-deprecating view of himself, once lamenting that a particularly earnest deceased comrade was "worth at least a half dozen soldiers such as me." Comer was wont to loaf off duty on occasion, boasting once about how he played off sick to obtain a ride in the surgeon's wagon rather than go on a tough march. He deserted in June 1863 while on the march to Tullahoma, and went home to visit his sick father, and then spent some time in the guard house at Tullahoma for his infraction. He remarked that by the end of his period of service, he was "from the hips down not reliable, but from there up, I am every particle O.K." Army records do not indicate if his medical condition rendered him unfit for service; but one charitably wonders that after partaking of the horrors of Bull Run, Shiloh, Stones River, Chickamauga, and Missionary Ridge, Comer couldn't take the killing any longer.

Little unfortunately is known of Comer's life before or after his wartime service. He was born February 24, 1836 in Lancaster, Ohio to Isaac and Anna (Cottrill) Comer, the second of six children. His oldest sister Lucretia died when Harry was three years old, and a family history indicates that his younger sibling John "disappeared as a child." The 1860 Federal census found him living with his family in Lancaster and working as a printer. In appearance, army records describe him as 5' 8 ½" tall with a dark complexion, grey eyes, and black hair. As the final letters of this collection indicate, Comer spent the ending months of the war in and out of hospitals and was listed as a deserter when his company mustered out on September 14, 1864. Comer's father died while he was in the army; his mother died in 1878 but Harry either did not or was unable to attend the funeral. It might be that Harry never recovered his health after the war- he died July 25, 1881 at the Hocking County Infirmary in Logan, Ohio and is buried there in an unmarked grave. He never married.

These are not the letters of a hero. But while Harry Comer might not have been a "model soldier," he proved to be a model correspondent, witty, observant, and chatty. The record he left via these letters serves to deepen our understanding of the tenor and timbre of the regular soldiers that comprised the Army of the Cumberland, and leave a very human record of that costliest of our wars.

Daniel A. Masters
March 2017

Private Harry Comer, Company A, 1st Ohio Volunteer Infantry (Abby Kitcher)

Chapter One

NINETY DAYS TO BULL RUN

Harrisburg Encampment, Pennsylvania
April 21, 1861

Up to the time we left Columbus for the eastern part of our trip, everybody must be acquainted with every move of our company. Starting out with a band of 109 men, able bodied, young, and vigorous, we presented at least a large appearance for the inland city; but one by one, we saw them drop off at Columbus, bid us farewell and depart. Since then, we have had the misfortune to lose two of our number from the ranks, one probably having been left by the transportation train, starting away while he was walking around Pittsburg. We are now reduced to 90 men, well-conditioned and in good order. Our encampment at present, for last night, today, and tonight, is the Senate Chamber of the State House, a fine building inside and out, but nothing to compare to the State House at Columbus, although the latter does look like a huge cabbage head upon which an owl has built its nest.

Among Company A are some as fine young men as can be found in the world; all taken from old Fairfield County, and mostly from Lancaster. Our Captain Joe Stafford thus far has exhibited no arrogance at all; clothed with authority, he has done his best to advance the drill of his company and considering the fact that we are mostly green hands with fire arms, having been taken from the peaceful avocations of life , from shoemaker shops, saddler shops, tailor shops, brick yards, stores, cigar shops, billiard rooms, law offices, farms, carpenter shops, railroads, butcher shops, and printing offices, we have progressed as rapidly as could be expected. Captain Joe, as he is familiarly called by the boys, puts on no superfluous airs, and physically and socially surpasses any of the band box soldiery who usually monopolize the offices to the exclusion of better men. Tommy Hunter, First Lieutenant, is quick to comprehend the orders of his captain and attends to the rear line and side columns with an assiduity worthy of his lineage. Ezra Ricketts, Second Lieutenant, has proved himself to be a gentlemen and a competent officer; he has refused the entreaties of relatives and urgent appeal of friends and went forth manfully to fight the battles of the country. The boys are all in excellent spirits, well satisfied with themselves and officers, but what the brave boys are yet to undergo, what trials they will pass through, what sufferings they will see, is only a matter of conjecture. Rest assured that the boys will acquit themselves with honor to themselves and relatives, and to the glory of the state of Ohio.

All is bustle and confusion today, among the masses that throng the State House yard to catch a glimpse of the various companies and regiments as they pass to and fro in their drilling exercises. Capt. Miller of Cincinnati became insane today from the effects of the excitement and was confined in the upper rooms of the capitol, but maintains his belligerence to us seceders from him by pelting us with stone coal and loaves of bread. Kitty Linn[1] has appointed himself commissary for the company and when meals are somewhat delayed, Kitty generally finds a way of getting eatables to the hungry. Ben Butterfield makes a good orderly sergeant and is well liked by the company, while our esteemed aid-de-camp to Capt. Stafford and gentleman-barber Joseph Hawkins keeps his eye skinned for breakers and watches things generally. The boys generally are in for one fight at least; some of them 'spilin' for a muss.'

"Night out" carries his head upright and philosophically, while all are in good health and have an abundance of nerve. Next week, after arriving at the field of battle, if living, I will again write you.

Weekly Lancaster Gazette, April 25, 1861, pg. 3

Lancaster, Pennsylvania
April 27, 1861

We are now snugly encamped at this place and have been here since last Tuesday morning, where we have very snug quarters to sleep in and quite good grub, that is for soldiers! For sleeping apartments in this camp, named in honor of Gov. William Dennison of our state, we have an enclosure in the shape of a rough wooden building built by the county fair association, in which the boys have made bunks, found straw for feather beds and cover themselves with blankets with which there were supplied at Camp Curtin near Harrisburg. Our grub is of the substantial kind; meat and bread for breakfast, bread and meat and water for dinner; cheese, coffee and bread for supper; for after- piece and dessert, we have whiskey smuggled into camp after our officers go to bed, peanuts and apples stolen from peanut peddlers as they go around with their baskets, and onions purloined from a neighboring farm house.

For amusements, we have recourse to several kinds and in this connection I may say that we have the best singers, the loudest hollowers, the best musicians, the most scientific card players, the quickest barber, the most sociable captain, the finest lieutenants, the quickest orderly sergeant, the best looking privates, and more fun than any other company of either the 1st or 2nd Ohio regiments now in this mammoth encampment. As an evidence of this, hundreds throng our quarters after the drilling exercises of the day are finished to hear the music of the captain's fiddle and see the dancing of the company. And when you attend, editors, another ball at City Hall and hear the music of your experienced and full cotillion bands, see fair women and superbly dressed men, and pay a visit for mint juleps and all the delicacies of the table which our native country can bring to bear upon a hungry stomach at the Tallmadge House, recollect that you ain't having all the fun; that we, in the camp, with the ground under us, are having a cotillion, too. That Joe and Ben are playing the violin and the company swinging partners with all the variations and callings in the way of 'swing partners,' 'ladies change,' 'gents the same,' etc.

There is one difference, however, between the suppers at our balls and the suppers at your balls. You probably, at your festivities, will have roast beef, pork, lamb, oysters, clams, sardines, fricassees, ice cream, lemonade, floats, strawberries, and melons. We'll have cold meat with fat on, meat in the bone, meat outside the bone, meat itself, square pieces of bread, bread in square pieces, zigzag pieces, pieces zigzag, angular pieces, triangular, quintupular, and sextupular. It will be a question likewise which of the two will have the most enjoyment. While you will be abundantly blessed with magnificent music and all the eatable delicacies of the season, blessed with the society of women, therein you have the advantage of us.; but we will be where no cold formality drives away enjoyment, where 'pitch in' is the order of the day, where true, whole-souled, hearty enjoyment supersedes cautious reserve of insidious formality.

Twenty-two miles from here is the town of York, where the bridges were burned down by the Baltimore mob and around which a strong guard of soldiers was placed to protect workmen while engaged in rebuilding them. Three fourths of a mile from here is Wheatland, the residence of James Buchanan, ex-president of what was once the United States and by the grace of God's will, stout arms and willing hearts, will be so again. About 50 of our boys went over to see the sage this morning. The old gentleman is a strong Union man in for its perpetuation, expressed himself satisfied with present movements and is no way fearful that Gen. Twiggs will execute his threat to visit summary punishment upon him for branding him a traitor and expelling him from the army.

Our boys are all well but one, in good spirits, fat, hale, and hearty, and have us down to 88 in number. Capt. Stafford is all we could wish him to be as commander of Company A, 1st Regiment Ohio Volunteers. The majorship of the regiment was proffered him by the captains of several companies who have a majority in the regiment, but his reply, spoken like a man and a soldier, "I came from the same place with my men. I am intimately acquainted with them; whatever they suffer, I suffer. Whatever they enjoy, I enjoy. I shall stick with them." This has endeared him more fully to his company than heretofore if possible.

When we leave here, where we'd go to, how much bread we'll get for dinner today, is merely a matter of conjecture, but one thing is certain; we would like to get papers and letters from home, but can't tell you where to direct.

Weekly Lancaster Gazette, May 9, 1861, pg. 1

Camp McClelland, near Philadelphia, Pennsylvania
May 8, 1861

We arrived in this city of cities on last Wednesday afternoon at 2 o'clock, and were marched from there to Camp McClelland distant seven miles from the city, which was formerly Suffolk Park, where G.M. Patchen, Lady Suffolk, Ethan Allen, Lexington, Flora Temple and Fire Fly, and a multitude of other famous trotting and running horses have astonished the sporting world and rivaled the time of Long Island.

We were carried at Lancaster for this place without lengthy notice, left there without any rations, missed our dinners, arrived in West Philadelphia at half past two, were marched here on an empty stomach, no message of our coming was telegraphed to this place and of course we had no supper, and so, half famished for food, we vamoosed through holes in the fence, crawled over the enclosure, broke through the gate guards, tired and hungry as we were, and made our way to town, where the news of our bad treatment or the gross negligence of the commissary (call it what you may) had reached them, and we were plenteously supplied by the Quaker City's hospitable citizens with an abundance of provisions. Philadelphia is indeed a city of brotherly love.

We had been hungry, tired, and sleepy, and some probably sick at heart, but not one of us now regret the necessity which impelled us to revolt against military rule and run the gauntlet of a discharge from the army; for, of all the cities in the world, American or foreign, a mind like mine cannot conceive how any place can have better or more hospitable citizens, prettier pavements, cleaner streets, more loyalty to the Union, more patriotic members of the former dark days of the Republic, or any other than can lay claim with more propriety to the affectionate title of the city of brotherly love. All hail the arch of the Keystone!

Here are to be seen some gorgeous palatial private residences, hotels that rival in beauty and splendor the famous bizarres of olden time; mercantile houses with mammoth marble fronts stretching backwards and forwards over mountains of silks, satins, calicos, linens, woolen goods, and notions. Carpenter's Hall, where as early as 1724 a declaration of independence was attempted to be drafted, where the Reverend Duchey of France prayed with the inspiration of heaven in him, where the 35th Psalm was read, and where old John Adams was supposed to have said "Live or die, sink or swim, survive or perish, I give my heart and hand to this vote;" where Benjamin Franklin wrote and published his philosophical essays; the Masonic Hall with its incomparable and unexcellable interior apartments and fixtures; where Washington was High Priest, Adams King, and Hancock Scribe; where, at the Navy Yard, can be seen those missiles of death in the shape of cannon from 10 pounders to 168 pounders, carbines, Minie rifles, breech loading mongrels, grape, canister, and bomb shells without number, etc. About 300 yards out in the Delaware River is that staunch old Union ship, the *U.S.S. Princeton* once commanded by Commodore Stockton, the Union flag still floating at her mast head and her top sails reefed with Union emblems. Across the bay is the city of monopolies, Camden, New

Jersey where our boys were taken prisoners the moment they landed and wild duck, fresh fish, and salad were shot into them by a vicious landlord. But it would take months to enumerate all of the sights seen by one unaccustomed to the beauties of a mammoth city whose populations number at present over 600,000 white people. Suffice it to say that the Continental Hotel covers up almost a Philadelphia block.

But the grandest sight that inspires enthusiasm and brings with it the most pleasurable recollections is Independence Hall. The flag of our common country is flying at its top and as you enter the center and turn to the left, you open a door and then stand in a room where the Declaration of Independence was adopted, where the patriot sages of the revolution convened and made this the birth place (as Faneuil Hall is the cradle) of American liberty. Around the walls of the room are the portraits of the signers of that immortal instrument which will carry their names down to the remotest posterity, to the 'latest syllable of recorded time' associated with them are several Indian chiefs who have been friendly to the whites in days gone by; Lafayette, Kosciusko, Red Jacket, and all the prominent men who pledged their lives in 1776, 1812, and 1846 for their country's welfare.

Around the statue of Washington, in the rear, are some revolutionary curiosities, a bottle of flattened shape dug from the earth at a distance of 80 feet, a 15 shilling note on brown paper of the old Continental money resembling a castor oil label in a state of decomposition, and a piece of live oak in which the charter was hidden from the Tories. To the right of the statue in a pedestal is the old Independence Bell which first rang out our national chimes and 'proclaimed liberty to all the inhabitants thereof.' The old bell has now a mammoth crack in it and some marks in it from people picking at it with knives in order to get a particle as a memento, but it is none the less reverenced on that account.

We leave here shortly but direct papers and letters to us at Philadelphia as arrangements are made with postmasters to send everything after us.

Weekly Lancaster Gazette, May 16, 1861, pg. 3

Washington City, District of Columbia
May 27, 1861

Nothing of unusual note occurred at Philadelphia since my last communication on the state of affairs with the solitary exception of my surprise in the Philadelphia mint. Robert Shannon, Jesse Weeks, Asa Nichols and myself (the four literary boys in Company A, 1st Regt. O.V.M.) made a visit a short time before our departure to that institution and were shown through by a humane old man with whitened locks who did his utmost to give us information in the art of making money in the literal sense of the word. First we came to the penny department when nickel and copper mingle together; next silver, where silver is properly adulterated with ink; lastly, where brown nickel blends together with the precious metal gold- all of it legitimized counterfeiting. The various processes through which these metals in the rough pass before they come out in good order and ready for disbursement I have not time in this letter to tell, because I know nothing about it, suffice it to say that I had in my hands eight pieces of gold in bars valued at $1,400 apiece! Saw pieces of standard money of all the states and principalities of the world from the eight square or octagon American $50 piece down to the Indian wampum; saw bullion enough to sink the *Leviathan* or *Great Eastern*,[2] and dreamed of golden eagles, cords of silver, mountains of bullion, etc. for a week; imagined myself a Montezuma eating golden bread, sleeping on golden bedsteads but just as I would reach out my hand to scatter alms to the poor, I would awaken and find my hand in fat pork and sea biscuit, navy bread, and bomb proof crackers! I am now poor once more.

I was sadly disappointed in Washington City's appearance. Expecting to see in this city of 'magnificently magnificent distances' a place the like of which had never been seen before, a place to dazzle the eye and enthuse the heart; one that would create surprise and admiration in a youthful bosom. I found it in every way inferior to Dayton and far from rivaling Columbus. The Capitol building is truly a grand mass of excellent marble, well put together and all in all a magnificent structure. The innumerable historical paintings which line the walls of the Rotunda, the portraits of eminent men who have served the Union by sword and speech and pen bring beautiful reminiscences to our minds; the statues in the niches remind us of that proud defiance which 'Greece and Rome in better ages knew,' the marble forms of Washington, Boone, and Christopher Columbus enjoin us to keep in dear remembrance those who won by sword, by pen, by firm determination to ask for nothing but what was right and to submit to nothing wrong the liberty we now enjoy. The Patent Office is a sight worth seeing. There can be found all the curiosities in the ways of patents ever invented, from a darning needle by Haddock to one of Hoe's[3] last fast six cylinder presses. The Post Office department is situated in a splendid building also, as indeed are the other Federal departments.

At least 40,000 troops are here and that many more in close marches from the city. We are quartered one and a half miles from town, several side steps to the left from us is the 2nd Ohio regiment; 1,000 paces 'rear rank open order' is the New York 79th, left obliquely is the Connecticut regiment, the Rhode Island on the brow of the hill 400 yards distant, to the front and center are the Jersey Blues. When these and us with the innumerable hordes in close proximity will 'close in mass' I do not know but we were all in arms on Friday last to march to the demolition of Alexandria and Sewell's Point after the murder of Col. Ellsworth.[4] The order was rescinded before we crossed the river.

Some of Company A may never live to get home, perhaps none, but rest assured whilst here we will do our best, trusting to a kind Providence who doeth all things well that our lives may be spared to return to fathers, mothers, brothers, sisters, wives, sweethearts, relatives, and friends in the good old country of Fairfield. B.F. Connell is here and has done his best to make our stay pleasant. He is in the Treasury department, comptroller's office. I saw here yesterday a roll of butter and a clean shirt- they didn't belong to our company.

Weekly Lancaster Gazette, June 6, 1861, pg. 3

Camp Sherman, Washington, D.C.
June 1, 1861

The boxes of goods, chattels, pies, cakes, money, stockings, cigars, tobacco, radishes, onions, canned fruit, shirts, handkerchiefs, towels, and liquids of various kinds arrived accompanied with dear letters from fathers, mothers, sisters, brothers, wives, relatives, friends and sweethearts on Thursday evening last, and to the say that the boys forgoed the doubtful felicity of supping on fat pork and navy bread spiced with dishwater coffee would be superfluous; be it sufficient to state that the boys 'pitched in' devouring all, even to the paper in which various edibles and valuables were wrapped- not however, at one meal, but if any one, however sharp-sighted or to whatever tension his optics might be stretched, could find a stray crumb in the morning, his vision is considerably more acute than that of any member of Company A. You ought to have seen the tables on which we ate our delicacies. Some were on the fence crosswise, dried beef in one hand, pound cake in the other, others got up into the trees singing 'Oh, who in the dickens would not love to roam, when vittles like these are sent us from home!'

Some of our high officers such as file closers, cooks, camp cleaners, corporals and sergeants absolutely got cheese and fruit cake, and you ought to have seen the poor privates who got nothing but ginger snaps, jumbles, mince pies, raisins, figs, fruit, and pound cake envying them! Ben Butterfield and Ezra Ricketts went out in a foot and a half mud hole and stood on their heads with a jar of pickles and a crock of butter as file leaders to their mouths and the last seen of Capt. Stafford, he and Joe Hawkins were about a mile from camp (having crawled through a hole in the fence made by Jesse Weeks) diving right hastily into the large cake sent by the Odd Fellows; they were in a fence corner, using pieces of the fence stake for knives and looking lovingly at each other as pound by pound of 'friendship, love, and truth' took its melancholy passage down the great gateway of pork, beans, and lager beer! Lieutenant Hunter must have gorged himself to death as he has not been seen since; several bottles of – also came to hand, but as the members of Company A, like the members of Captain Stinchcomb's company are temperance men, the bottles were immediately smashed and the contents thrown down.

In this connection, I must tender my thanks together with those of the whole company for the many kind little tokens of remembrance received, all the more valuable because coming from home, the home of our childhood, where all who are near and dear to us reside and where, when we die, we wish our remains to be buried. Many tokens and symbols to remind us of what we received are distributed around our tents in the shape of autobiographical sentiments, such as to 'To William, from he knows who,' or 'To James from his sister Caroline and Mary,' or "To John from his affectionate mother.' Here and there can be seen empty fruit cans, empty cigar boxes, ruffled tin foil, etc. My reminder is in the shape of three One Dollar Williams State Bank of Ohio, received from some of the best fellows the world ever saw. I have opened a side show with them in my tent, admission 10 cents, soldiers half price. Charles Fields and Kit Linn, agents. It is called the 'Cabinet of Astounding Curiosities!'

Hugh Daugherty returned to camp today having got over a severe attack of pneumonia. Everybody is well, good-looking, fat, ragged, sassy, full of fun, frolic, devilment, and in for one battle, if it is only to whip the 2nd Regiment, so they say, but I am opposed to any such foolishness as I have acted more philosophically since getting whipped at Logan by a fellow I thought I could whip, but who whipped me! A heavy guard of sentinels are placed around every camp and picket guards are placed at a distance of three miles around us; but notwithstanding these precautions, every nigger seen at night, every white man seen in daytime, and every cow and house is supposed to be a secessionist in disguise and the cry, crisply spoken, of "Halt! Advance and give the countersign!" turns many a Negro white, many a white man blue, and drives away innumerable cows.

Rumor has it that we start for Virginia this afternoon, but as old rumor had lied upon several occasions, I think we would not lose a great deal by disbelieving her until we are further advised. One things is certain however; large bodies of men and going into Virginia, for something or other, which time will demonstrate. I have no more news to give you and will therefore close, as my letter was merely to be a surety to your mind that the boxes from home had been received and duly disposed of. May I be able to record another acknowledgement before long. Since writing the above, Lt. Hunter has made his appearance in tolerable good health, having taken an emetic and got well of his gorged condition, consequent on eating too many of the delicacies sent us. He requests me to send his compliments to you and yours. When anything more transpires worthy of note, I shall write you.

Weekly Lancaster Gazette, June 6, 1861, pg. 3

Pine Hill Camp, Fairfax Co., Virginia
June 16, 1861

We are, after a considerable lapse of time, in northeastern Virginia within five miles of Fairfax Courthouse and within a quarter mile of the former camp of the Fire Zouaves, once under command of the lamented Col. Ellsworth. We left our quarters near Washington City on Wednesday morning and after a march or two or three miles arrived at another rendezvous, between hills and in hollows where rivulets flowed and shade trees beckoned, and the silvery notes of the woodland songsters were continually wafted to our ears, where beautiful springs gushed up from many grottoes and nature had done a work which art itself could only blemish. Here, coming to the conclusion that fortune had at last favored us, we were well contented and passed the time in tripping up and down the meandering stream, rudely standing under the many cascades or rollicking in the shade, but our joy was merely transitory. We had too much happiness to suit his obesity Col. McCook!

The order to pitch tents was given and at 9 o'clock we took up our march for some place or the other, which it was expected we would reach some time or the other. It was 10 o'clock at night when we arrived at a large field on the Alexandria pike about five miles from Washington in which we encamped and I, being a component part of the 'third relief,' was placed on duty in the center of a two acre swamp near the Potomac River. Here as a sentry, I walked my lonely beat with my eye peeled and my heart fluttering until 5 o'clock in the morning. This was our first bivouac which means walking a long distance after bed time on a sandy road, having had no supper, laying down in the open air on your luggage, consisting of two suits of clothes, what old clothes you brought from home and wish to still retain, a large field coat, an extra hat, a zinc canteen filled with water, a haversack with plates, knives, forks, and provisions, and large double blanket, a knapsack, cap box, belt, a cartridge box (heavily loaded), and a 14 lb musket- all these on your back and then drop down on the bare ground with the canopy of heaven above you-that is called a bivouac.

In the morning at 5, the reveille sounded, all raised in quick order (1st and 2nd regiments) and came by a fatiguing march here where one day's rations failed and for four meals the boys got nothing but what they brought with them and that was precious little. Some were forced out to scouting and came across a flouring mill where the proprietor was absent. Corn and wheat were procured, the water turned on, a practical miller from Mansfield set the machinery to motion, grists were ground and flour and corn meal in an unbolted condition soon found its way to our regiment.

We are in 'Extra' Billy Smith's [5] congressional district, a strong hold of secessionism and where double guards are necessarily placed around our battalions. Everything is under martial law; persons seized and searched, passes minutely examined, strict vigils kept, and all caught after 9 o'clock at night, arrested or shot. Troops of the Confederacy in large numbers are now at Manassas Junction and there is where we expect to meet them. All of us are well but have not yet received pay. 'We get it tomorrow,' so I have heard for the last two weeks, but the pay we received may reach us in paradise for the battle, bloody and relentless, which will inevitably soon take place and drench our land in fraternal blood, the like of which the world never saw, and of which, in point of ferocity, Napoleon never dreamed. The first foes met by us will be a set of as desperate cut throats, thieves, robbers, blacklegs and murderers as ever disgraced this country; but after they are beaten, as in the wisdom of God there surely will be, our final victory may be easy, but many a brave boy has seen his last of home and its joys-possibly the last of earth soon. Affairs are coming to a crisis soon, but all are waiting for that second donation from home, hoping it may come on the night of a great battle, when the Union troops have been successful and Capt. Stafford's company can still count its full number of men and each answer at roll call to his name. God grant it may be so!

P.S. Send letters and papers to Washington City, as couriers go there every day with wagons.

Weekly Lancaster Gazette, June 27, 1861, pg. 3

Camp Upton, Fairfax Co., Virginia
July 11, 1861

This is, most probably, the last emanation of mine from camp to the reading public of Fairfield. By this time next week, if not placed as targets by Brig. Gen. Schenk before that time or turned loose to seek whom we may devour, we will be in Columbus or at home. This will be a severe blow to the literati of Lancaster, a cause of deep sorrow to the editors of the *Gazette* and a source of financial depression to the paper maker; for, modest and unassuming as I am, I know full well that I write a very sensible letter, express my ideas in terse and elegant language, combine all the qualities of pathos, sarcasm, irony, imagination, pithiness, in fact all the qualities essential to a first class contributor to a first class family and literary paper.

Nothing of note has transpired since I last wrote you except the arrival of the provision boxes from home, the eating of contents thereof, the arrival of Dr. Scott, the visit to our camp of Hocking H. Hunter, Esq. Harry getting broke at a chuck-a-luck table, the convening of the Congress of the United States, and my peep at the 'notables' in Washington, among whom were old Abe, generals of every grade, Winfield Scott, Chase, Seward, Cameron, Wells, Bates, Blair, Smith, John B. Weller, William Russell, Emerson Etheridge, Bob Clarke of the *Lancaster Gazette*, and some smaller lights unworthy of mention.

Next Wednesday the 17th inst. our time of military service is up. Taking a retrospective glance at men, manners, and circumstances we have had much to gratify and interest us and a little that did not. We didn't like to stand out rainy nights on guard, march in the hot sun through miles of soggy sand, bear the insolence of red tape officials without merit, live on swill slop and pilot bread, didn't like McCook's battalion drills, our scrape at Vienna, or the unplethoric condition of a month-a go's pocket books. Neither did we fancy the prodigious rains that sent aqueous torrents through our flimsy tents or the first lot of 'regimentals' given to us by our uncle. Several other little items were disagreeable to persons of such refined sensibilities as those of Company A, 1st Regt. O.V.M. But we did like the friendly visit of H.B. Hunter to our camp in Lancaster, Pennsylvania; the presents of figs, raisins, and canned peaches from Andrew Reid; the revolvers sent us by A.J. Dildine; the proffer of the majorship of the regiment to Capt. Stafford at Harrisburg, his refusal of the same; the diversified beauties of nature to be seen in the rolling prairies, level lawns, mountainous ranges, golden sunsets, fairy grottoes, murmuring streams, dashing cascades, blue-tipped bays, and many a natural curiosity, wonder and beauty that will never be effaced from our memories, the souvenirs from home in the shape of letters and the provisions sent us in goodly times were a source of exceeding joy.

Our regimental officers Col. McCook, Lt. Col. Parrott, Major Hughes, Adjutant Parrott, Sergeant Major McKinney, and Fife Major Robinson are men of fine military qualities and well liked as officers. Brig. Gen. Schenk is esteemed as a man of large heart and fine mind, but not as a military man. Dropping down in grade to our company officers, we have never had cause to regret our enlistment under them. Capt. Joe Stafford is the same as when we first learned to love him and while others with far less military skill, less of hardihood and bravery, less of all that goes to make up a strict disciplinarian, competent commander and at the same time a gentleman; while others, who think a private has no rights which red tape is bound to respect, are putting on snobbish airs, doing the French and acting the puppy, he had brought a company of raw recruits to a greater degree of perfection than any other; made hundreds of friends in other companies, preserved by a kind solicitude, their welfare, the health of his men, gained the confidence of higher officers by meritorious deeds and at the same time frolicking with his men and when off duty considered himself no better. Lt. Hunter, Lt. Ricketts, and brevet Lt. Butterfield are as kind and sociable, as pert and jolly as ever and Company A wishes no better aids to Capt. Joe than them.

Now to the nub! We will be home soon; say this next week, when Capt. Stafford and Lt. Ricketts and Butterfield will be ready to receive recruits for three years' service. Anything asked by Capt. Stafford of the department will be immediately granted and the acceptance of the 1st and 2nd Ohio regiments is a foregone fact, granted in advance. Gen. Schenk, Col. McCook, and Lt. Col. Parrott have tendered him any position he chooses in the new regiment to be formed, the right, left, or color company, and those of Fairfield's boys who wish to 'march under the flag and keep step to the music of the Union,' to fight for the perpetuation of a Republican government, free speech, free presses and liberty; to vindicate at all times and under all circumstances the fact of our national existence; one who has not ties to bind him but patriotic zeal to urge him will find in camp life under Capt. Stafford as pleasing a soldier-life as falls the lot of anyone of whatever country or under whatever cause he is enlisted.

You, who like me, have nothing to bind them at home but parents and other members of the family whose consent can be readily obtained, enlist under Stafford; you who have lady loves, do likewise for when you return from the wars, covered in glory, your 'flame' will meet you as a hero-lover; you who are eking out a miserable existence or sponging out the life blood of an aged father, enlist under Stafford; you who have contracted an almost uncontrollable thirst for liquor, enlist, for a camp where whiskey is prohibited will cure the disease; you that have become too lazy to do anything, enlist, for camp life, sleeping in the open air, getting up before sunrise, standing nights in an enemy's country where you are compelled to be spry and a battalion drill with McCook as colonel and Stafford as captain-McCook to scold and Stafford to coax- will inevitably cure you of sluggishness. Enlist under the banner of beauty and glory, let it not be said you were 'invisible in peace, invisible in war' or 'soldiers in peace, in war citizens.'

Weekly Lancaster Gazette, July 18, 1861, pg. 3

Major General Alexander McDowell McCook, original commander of the 1st Ohio Volunteer Infantry and the general under which the 1st Ohio served throughout most of the war. The highest ranking member of the noted "Fighting McCooks," Alexander served as a brigade, division, and corps commander in the Army of the Cumberland before being relieved of command in the wake of the debacle at Chickamauga. (Library of Congress)

First Battle of Bull Run, Virginia
July 21, 1861

Washington City, D.C.
July 24, 1861

Since writing to you last, stirring scenes and startling events have transpired. Leaving Camp Upton at 2 p.m. on Friday July 15, with bright hopes of a speedy reunion with friends and relatives, we joined regiment after regiment, brigade after brigade, division after division until the grand army of occupation, filed in ranks of four numbering 50,000 men were marching toward Manassas Junction, the bands playing national airs, banners floating in the breeze, voices singing Union anthems, and myriad bayonets gleaming in the sun. Hugh and sanguine hopes were entertained that the horde of political blacklegs, bankrupt politicians, refugees from foreign climes and crimes, murderers, thieves, pick pockets and assassins who composed the Southern Rebel army would be most effectually wiped out and the Stars and Stripes float in glory and beauty o'er Vienna Station, Germantown, Fairfax Court House, Manassas Gap and Junction, and at last have a crowning glory by waving in majesty and beauty on the Capitol at Richmond. The station at Vienna was taken possession of, our national emblem placed on the track where one month before the 1st Ohio was fired into by a masked battery of the enemy. Germantown, Fairfax, and Centreville fell before the stern front and steady march of the army of freedom until we brought up at the northern fork of Bull Run on July 20. Here a masked battery within an entrenchment was stormed but with ill success, and both sides got off with considerable loss.

Sunday morning dark and early, 2 o'clock, our column under the command of Gen. McDowell marched to the since scene of conflict; Schenk's Brigade, composed of the 1st and 2nd Ohio regiments and the 2nd New York, was given the post of honor and were thrown out as advance skirmishers in order to detect and draw forth the enemy's fire of the masked batteries. The enemy lay strongly entrenched in unseen trenches under cover of the woods and in the long grass. The 1st Ohio made the opening charge of musketry, the 2nd New York followed at a double quick which brought forth the enemy's fire and regiment of riflemen who were finely repelled by the 2nd Ohio. Our brigade loss was comparatively small considering the dangerous position assigned us and as you have heard by the newspapers, telegraphic reports and rumors probably more than I know of the details, I leave the matter to the official report of our very worthy and efficient brigadier who has, after a considerable lapse of time and by keeping us boys over their time, avenged the slaughter of Vienna and gained a reputation for Ohio.

The battle of Bloody Run will never be effaced from the O.V.M.'s memory; the mounds of dead and dying, the heroic charges, the rivers of blood, the death groans of comrades, the ghastly visage, the faintly articulated cry for water, the bombs bursting, the cannon's flash, the impetuous rush, the Grecian stolidity, the Roman courage, the army of enthusiastic, impetuous, devoted and courageous soldiers who rushed into the jaws of death and charged into the cannon's mouth will live vividly in their memories long after the Rebels who caused the disaster and death have expired their crimes by an ignominious death of earth, and a torturing life among the spirits of the damned!

The precipitate retreat, the hurried flight from the field of action, was owing to a misconstrued order and it is estimated that 15,000 U.S. troops were in close proximity that were not in the engagement at all. Up to 3 p.m., the battle was ours when Johnston's Rebel reinforcements turned the tide and compelled a retreat which, although not compulsory, was a necessity. We were ordered to retreat which we lost time in doing and starting at the double quick came a distance of over 30 miles, our muskets, canteens, blankets, haversacks, cartridge boxes, etc. still a component of our baggage. At Fort Corcoran, Arlington Heights, we were kept in a drenching rain for six mortal hours while regiment after regiment moved past us to shelter, food, and repose. We are now here in Washington City, barracked at Union Block, corner of 6th and Pennsylvania Avenue, while your correspondent has taken rooms at the Avenue House, doffed his soldier clothes, donned clean toggery, and imagines himself once more a citizen!

The order has been given to march to camp at 10 o'clock today at the end of 7th Street to attend to roll call and see who are killed, wounded, and missing, and to make arrangements for getting home as soon as troops now in waiting for orders are marched to this city to fill our places. L.M. Dayton and Myron H. Gregory are here, together with Gen. William T. Sherman of our city, who was commandant of a brigade. Company A has lost none of its members with possibly the exception of William Swigert[6] who was substituted in place of Kitty Linn as a pioneer. He has not yet reported himself at headquarters.

Weekly Lancaster Gazette, August 1, 1861, pg. 3

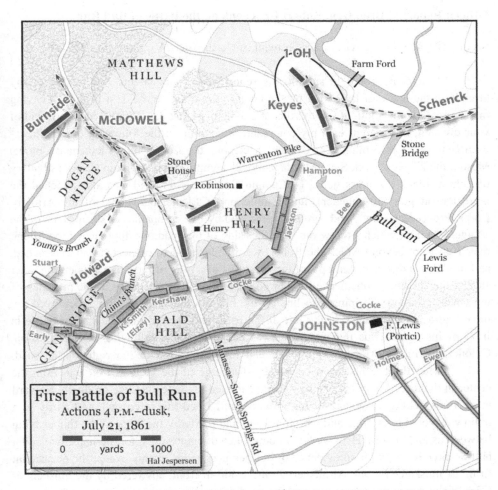

The First Battle of Bull Run, July 21, 1861. The 1st Ohio, part of Brig. Gen. Robert Schenk's three regiment brigade, maintained position near the Stone Bridge through most of the day and was but lightly engaged. The regiment's primary service at Bull Run was in covering the retreat of the army back to Washington, with regimental casualties being very light. Comer commented that the battle would be remembered "for the mounds of dead and dying, the heroic charges, the rivers of blood, the death groans of comrades, the ghastly visage, the faintly articulated cry for water, the booms bursting, and the cannon's flash." Map by Hal Jespersen. CWMaps.com

Official Report of Brig. Gen. Robert C. Schenk on the Battle of Bull Run

Second Brigade, First Division, Department of Northeastern Virginia, July 23, 1861

I have the honor to submit this report of the movements and service of my brigade in the battle of Bull Run, on the Gainesville road, on the 21st instant: Leaving my camp, one mile south of Centreville, at 2.30 a.m. of that day, I marched at the head of your division, as ordered, with my command in column, in the following order: The 1st Regiment of Ohio Volunteers, Colonel McCook; the 2nd Ohio, Lieutenant-Colonel Mason; the 2nd New York State Militia, Colonel Tompkins, and Captain Carlisle's battery of light artillery, six brass guns. To Captain Carlisle's command was also attached the large Parrott gun (30-pounder), under direction of Lieutenant Hains, of the Artillery Corps. Proceeding slowly and carefully, preceded by five companies of skirmishers of the 1st and 2nd Ohio, which I threw out on either side of the road, we approached the bridge over Bull Run, beyond which the Rebels were understood to be posted and entrenched, and to within a distance, perhaps, of three-fourths of a mile of their batteries on the other side of the stream. In obedience to your command, on first discovery of the presence of the enemy's infantry forming into line on the hill-side beyond the Run, I deployed my three regiments of infantry to the left of the road, and formed them in line of battle in front of his right. Thus my command was constituted--the left wing of our division, Colonel Sherman's brigade, coming up and taking position to the right of the road. After the fire had been opened by discharge of the large Parrott gun from the center in the direction of the enemy's work, I moved my extended line gradually forward at intervals, taking advantage of the ground, until I had my force sheltered partly in a hollow, covered by a ridge and wood in front, and partly by the edge of the timber lying between us and the run. Here we lay, in pursuance of your orders, for, perhaps, two and a half or three hours, with no evidence of our nearness to the enemy except the occasional firing of musketry by our skirmishers in the wood in front, answered by the muskets or rifles of the enemy, to whom our presence and position were thus indicated, with a view to distract his attention-from the approach of Col. Hunter's force from above and in his rear. At this time I received your notice and order announcing that Hunter was heard from, that he had crossed, and was coming down about two miles above us, and directing that if I saw any signs of a stampede of the enemy in front I should make a dash with the two Ohio regiments, keeping the New York regiment in reserve. For this movement I immediately formed and prepared. Soon after, and when, by the firing of artillery and musketry in front at the right, it appeared that the Rebels were actively engaged in their position by our forces on the other side of the stream, I received your order to extend my line still farther to the left, sending forward Col. McCook's regiment to feel the battery of the enemy, which was ascertained to be on the hill covering the ford, half a mile below the bridge, and supporting him with my two other regiments. This was immediately done.

Col. McCook advanced in that direction along the road, which we found to be a narrow track through a pine wood, thick and close with undergrowth, and flanked on either side by ambuscades of brush-work, which were now, however, abandoned.

Reaching the head of this narrow road where it opened upon the stream, Col. McCook found the battery to be a strong earthwork immediately opposite, mounted with at least four heavy guns, and commanding the outlet from the wood. An open space of hollow ground lay between, with a corn-field to the left, the direct distance across to the enemy's battery being about three hundred and fifty yards. Behind this battery, and supporting it, were discovered some four regiments of the Rebel troops, while rifle-pits were seen directly in front of it. The 1st Regiment was then deployed to the left in the edge of the woods and into the corn-field, one company (Captain John Kell's) being thrown forward towards the run up to within perhaps twenty yards of the battery.

While this was done I advanced the 2nd Ohio, followed by the 2nd New York, toward the head of the road, in supporting distance from the 1st Ohio, Lt. Col. Mason's regiment filing also to the left. Receiving Col. McCook's report of the battery, and that it would be impossible to turn it with any force we had, I immediately dispatched a message to the center to bring up some pieces of artillery, to engage the enemy from the head of the road. In the meantime the enemy, discovering our presence and position in the woods, and evidently having the exact range of the road we were occupying, opened on us with a heavy fire of shells and round and grape shot. To avoid the effect of this as much as possible, I ordered the men to fall back into the woods on each side of the road, and was presently re-enforced by two guns of Ayres' battery, under Lt. Ransom, which passed to the head of the road. A brisk cannonading was then opened, but a very unequal one, on account of the superior force and metal of the enemy. While this continued, I left my horse and passed through the woods, and remained some time by our guns, to be satisfied whether we were making any impression on the enemy's work. I soon found that it was not thus to be carried, and such also was the opinion of the officer in charge of the guns. Retiring, I found that the most of my two regiments in the rear had fallen back out of range of the hot and constant fire of the enemy's cannon, against which they had nothing to oppose. The suffering from this fire was principally with the 2nd New York, as they were in the line where most of the shell and shots fell that passed over the heads of the 2nd Ohio.

Taking with me two companies of the 2nd Ohio, which were yet in the woods maintaining their position, I returned to cover, and brought away Ransom's guns. It was just at this place and point of time that you visited yourself the position we were leaving. I must not omit to speak with commendation of the admirable manner in which these guns of ours were handled and served by the officers and men having them in charge; and I may notice the fact also that, as we were withdrawing from this point, we saw another heavy train of the enemy's guns arrive and move up the stream on the other side of their battery with which we had been engaged along what we supposed to be the road from Manassas towards where the battle was raging with our troops on the right.

My three regiments being all called in, then returned and rested in good order at the center of the front, near the turnpike. Here I was informed by Col. McCook that you had crossed the run above with other portions of our division, and left with him an order for me to remain with my infantry in that position supporting Carlisle's battery, which was posted close to the road on the right. This was about 1 o'clock p.m. Capt. Carlisle, while we thus rested, was playing with much apparent effect upon the enemy's works across the run with his two rifled pieces, as was also Lt. Hains with the large Parrott gun. Soon after, having successive and cheering reports, confirmed by what we could observe, of the success of our Army on the other side of the run, I discovered that bodies of the enemy were in motion, probably retreating to their right. To scatter these and hasten their flight I ordered into the road toward the bridge the two rifled guns, and had several rounds fired, with manifest severe effect. This, however, drew from the enemy's batteries again a warm and quick fire of shell and with rifled cannon on our position in the road, which continued afterwards and with little intermission, with loss of some lives again in my New York regiment, until the close of the fight.

While this was going on, Capt. Alexander, of the Engineer Corps, brought up the company of pioneers and axmen, which, with its officers and sixty men, had been entirely detailed from the regiments of my brigade, to open a communication over the bridge and through the heavy abatis which obstructed the passage of troops on our front beyond the run. To support him while thus engaged, I brought and placed on the road towards the bridge McCook's and Tompkins' regiments, detailing also and sending forward to the bridge a company of the 2nd New Yorkers, to cover the rear while cutting through the enemy's abatis. A second company from Lt. Col. Mason's command was also brought forward with axes afterwards, to aid in clearing the obstructions, and thus in a short time Capt. Alexander succeeded in opening a passage.

Capt. Carlisle's battery was now posted on the hill-side in the open field to the left of the road toward the bridge. Very soon after, some reverse of fortune appearing to have taken place with our troops on the other side, who were falling back up the run, it was discovered and reported to me that a large body of the enemy had passed over the stream below the bridge, and were advancing through a wood in the low grounds at our left, with an evident purpose to flank us. To intercept this movement, I ordered forward into the road still lower down two of Carlisle's brass howitzers, a few rounds from which, quickly served, drove the Rebels from the wood and back to the other side of the stream. It was not long after this that the unpleasant intelligence came of our Army being in retreat from the front across the ford above, and the order was given to fall back on Centreville. The retreat of my brigade, being now in the rear of our division, was conducted in the reverse order of our march in the morning, the 2nd New York moving first, and being followed by the 2nd Ohio and 1st Ohio, the two latter regiments preserving their lines in good degree, rallying together and arriving at Centreville with closed ranks, and sharing comparatively little in the panic which characterized so painfully that retreat, and which seemed to me to be occasioned more by the fears of frightened teamsters, and of hurrying and excited civilians (who ought never to have been there), than even by the needless disorder and want of discipline of straggling soldiers.

Near the house which was occupied as a hospital for the wounded, about a mile from the battle-ground, a dashing charge was made upon the retreating column by a body of secession cavalry, which was gallantly repelled, and principally by two companies of the 2nd Ohio, with loss on both sides. Here also, in this attack, occurred some of the casualties to the 2nd New York Regiment. From this point to Centreville a portion of the 1st Ohio was detailed, under command of Lt. Col. Parrott, and acted efficiently as a rear guard, covering the retreat.

Arrived at Centreville, I halted the two Ohio regiments on the hill, and proceeded to call on Gen. McDowell, whom I found engaged in forming the reserve of the Army and other troops in line of battle to meet an expected attack that night of the enemy at that point. I offered him our services, premising, however, that unfed and weary troops, who had been seventeen hours on the march and battle-field, might not be very effective, unless it were to be posted as a reserve in case of later emergency. Gen. McDowell directed me to take them to the foot of the hill, there to stop and encamp. This I did, establishing the two regiments together in the wood to the west of the turnpike. After resting here about two hours, I was notified that your division, with the rest of the forces under the general commanding, were leaving Centreville, and received your order to fall back on Washington. I took the route by Fairfax Court-House, and thence across to Vienna, arriving at the latter place at 3.30 a.m. of the 22nd, and there resting the troops for two hours in an open field. During the march we did what was possible to cover the rear of the scattered column then on the road.

Two miles, or less, this side of Vienna, Col. McCook, with the main body of his regiment, turned upon the road leading to the Chain Bridge over the Potomac, thinking it might be a better way, and at the same time afford by the presence of a large and organized body protection to any stragglers that might have taken that route. Lt. Col. Mason, with the 2nd Ohio, marched in by the way of Falls Church and Camp Upton.

The return of the Ohio regiments to Washington was made necessary by the fact that, their term of service having expired, they are at once to be sent home to be mustered out of service.

Not having been able to obtain yet complete or satisfactory returns of all the casualties in the battle in the different corps of my brigade, I shall reserve the list of them for a separate report, which I will furnish as soon as practicable.

I remain your obedient servant,
ROBT C. SCHENK
Brigadier-General.

Chapter Two

A WINTER IN KENTUCKY, 1861-62

Camp Corwin, Dayton, Ohio
August 29, 1861

We arrived in this, the most beautiful city in Ohio, on Friday the 23rd, took breakfast at half past nine at the Montgomery House, from whence we started to camp situated two and half miles from the city. The ground was selected expressly for this purpose by Col. McCook and is one of the best and most practicable places for an encampment in the state. It is situated on a rolling hillock on high and extremely healthy land, where a beautiful spring of cool water gushes up from the foot and where a nice grove with its shadowy plumes and gentle breezes drives away dull care and lures us on to balmy repose. As yet, but four companies have made their report to headquarters but a dozen recruiting officers have the star spangled banner floating from their windows, all vying with each other as to who shall get their companies filled first in order to get into McCook's regiment, well knowing that such an accomplished officer, as Col. McCook is known to be, will not sacrifice the life of his men without making a desperate effort, aided by cool judgment, to prevent it. The companies now here are the following: Co. A Capt. Stafford, Co. B Capt. Kuhlman of Dayton, Co. C Capt. Thruston of Dayton, Co. D Capt. Ainswell of Cleveland (the Cleveland Grays). Here is a list of members of Co. A:

List omitted (see roster at end of book) but Comer lists himself as "1ˢᵗ Sergeant" while Solomon E. Homan was listed as 'orderly sergeant.' Comer was commissioned as Second Sergeant.

We have also at Zanesville ten men who have not made their appearance but have given assurances that they will. More of interest in my next.

Weekly Lancaster Gazette, September 5, 1861, pg. 3

Camp Corwin, Dayton, Ohio
September 8, 1861

Since writing to you, nothing of very great importance has transpired in camp. As yet, Company A has not lost any of its exuberance of spirits and as lively devils, I think they will compare favorably with the first Company A. More than half of our boys are from the country, are trained to rely on their own resources, have good honest hearts, but lack the vim and shrewdness of the old boys. Ten new men have joined our company since I made my list for you who came from home. Jim Gordon has not yet made his appearance. The new members are John F. Brown, Jeremiah Dennis, W. Groves, Riley Willison, David Road, John A. Shannon, John H. Manler, Benjamin Reber, George W. Reber, and Samuel P. Dinsmore, all good stout men who will make excellent soldiers.

We have 108 men and are the only company that reached the maximum standard now in camp here. Seven companies (one or two skeleton) are here but Company A in point of good looking men, stout built men, good captain, good lieutenants and first class sergeants wipes out anything in this part of the state, although 16 recruiting offices are now in the city of Dayton. All the excitement in this section at present is the stupendous arrangements now going forward preparatory to the state fair and the furor created in the crinoline kingdom whenever mess number two goes to town. Chuckaluck boards, dice, horse blankets, rot gut whiskey, tangle-leg beer, center poles, steamboat paste boards, ropes, flying Dutchmen, ginger cakes, and stoga cigars can been seen in all directions and the activity and bustle shows that this state fair will equal if not excel any of the former ones. The fair grounds are situated on the right hand side foot of Main Street one of the most beautiful spots of land in Montgomery County, a county noted for eligible sites and beautiful scenery.

We are to be marched into Dayton and out to the ground on Thursday next either by squad, company, or battalion and it is more than likely that a person with such shirkish proclivities as myself will find some excuse for breaking ranks and taking a peep at the sights and scenery, bars and bottles, gals, and girls. In such an event I shall write you the incidents and endeavor to give you what my eyes observe for which no doubt you will be abundantly grateful. Some saw we are to go to Camp Dennison near Cincinnati as it has been made a camp of instruction; others say we are to stay here to form a brigade with the other regiments to compose McCook's command. Our destination after we are thoroughly drilled is alike uncertain; some say Kentucky to drive away the Tennessee marauders who are endeavoring by armed bands to precipitate a loyal state out of the Union; others say that we go to Missouri to join the gallant Fremont, others say we are going to western Virginia to take in the Accomack orator and dog leg tobacco chewer Henry A. Wise., pseudo general. Others wish, among the number myself, that we may go again into eastern Virginia where the bloody battle of Manassas is to be completed with chain shot variations. The battle which must ere long commence in that locality will be bloody and relentless. They are strongly fortified, well posted, know every inch of the ground, have the best arms in use, are determined to conquer by fair or foul means with a preference for the latter as desperate from their consciousness of waning power and steadily augmenting strength of the Union forces, the battle to be fought is their last chance and although it may prevent a rise in the price of hemp if they are not beaten, it will only prolong the strife and render the feud more bitter and lasting.

Most of us are now peace men and in for compromise that is, in this way; let the Rebels lay down their arms and implements of warfare, give back the valuables stolen from the U.S. Mint at New Orleans, repair the damage done to the *Star of the West*, pay to the government the expenses of time, ammunition, damages, repairs etc. at the time of Sumter's bombardment; pay for the demolition of Gosport Navy Yard and all other expenses incident to the war and return to loyalty, then we are in favor of peace. Do this and then give up the head leaders of the Rebellion and there will be peace.

P.S. The United States will furnish its own hemp rope. My letter is getting lengthy. I'll close.

Weekly Lancaster Gazette, September 19, 1861, pg. 1

Camp Corwin, Dayton, Ohio
September 21, 1861

The Ohio State Fair is over and passed off in the usual style, not equaling as a state affair several I have heretofore witnessed and enjoyed. To be sure there was any amount of 'here's your great natural living curiosities-admittance 15 cents, the wild tigers stuffed with straw, the Maltese children 9 feet 8 inches high and the celebrated Lilliputs from Borneo, here's the only exhibition on the ground showing how prize battles are lost and won, and what figures do you bet on?' Lots and gobs of groceries (to use an exceedingly homely phrase) were on the grounds, in, around, and about them-places where posters were pasted notifying the passers-by that "no intoxicating liquors should be sold on the grounds,' but still a person of prying disposition of your correspondent imagined he saw diverse and sundry individuals sipping a life-like resemblance to various fluids known by the name of beer, ale, wine, whiskey, gin, brandy, schnapps, etc. Fine Art Hall and Floral Hall together with Mechanic, Domestic, and Vegetable Halls were well represented but in other departments there was a decided deficiency both in quality and quantity. The ladies and soldiers (the Lord bless them both) turned out in goodly numbers to see the sights and to be seen and were of course in their favorite elements- the ladies liking us, we liking the ladies. But as femininity is a subject I never like to write about, I close on the subject without telling how one of our lieutenants fell in love with a strange woman, or how the captain of Co. A was surrounded by Union Rebels in crinoline, or how Bob Shannon got lost in the woods, or how Jack Reed lost his breast pin, nor why Joe Groff goes to town so often.

Our food here is as good as we could wish; beef, good fresh bread with coffee, sugar, and potatoes for breakfast; beef, bean soup, potatoes and bread for dinner; ham, potatoes, bread and coffee for supper. Added to this, the boys frequently get things from home which as a general thing are divided among our own individual messmates. The citizens of Dayton have exhibited every feeling of kindness for us and frequent presents of peaches, pies, cakes, grapes, apples and beer are sent to us, which of course are not permitted to spoil in our hands.

We have five company drills per day, making a total of about six and half hours of drill. So we do 'bully' and other times not quite so 'bully.' No battalion drills have as yet been inaugurated the regiment not being full. Ten companies are here however some are not quite full: Co. A of Lancaster Capt. Stafford, Co. B of Dayton Capt. Kuhlman, Co. C of Dayton Capt. Thruston, Co. D of Cleveland Capt. Hanson, Co. E of Dayton Capt. O'Connell, Co. F of Miamisburgh Capt. Pomeroy, Co. G of Bellefontaine Capt. Trapp, Co. H of Cincinnati Capt. Lamison, Co. I of Columbiana County Capt. Snodgrass, and Co. K of Piqua Capt. Lawton. Most of them are strong, vigorous, young men, fighting for a principle and not profit, although I may say that the best paying positions are eagerly sought after. We have 775 men enrolled and sworn into service for three years or during the war who are now here while some 150 others are enrolled on different company lists who are expected but have not yet come. 830 is the minimum number for a regiment but Col. McCook wishes this to reach the maximum (1,010) of infantry with a company of cavalry and six pieces of artillery. Our regimental officers are Col. A. McDowell McCook, Lt. Col. Edwin A. Parrott, Major E. Bassett Langdon, Adjutant J.M. Lenhard, Sergeant Major Patterson, Quartermaster James Hill; most of them formerly of the 1st regiment of three months' troops, men of intelligence, who know their business, and intend to do it.

In my first letter to you from Camp Corwin, there were a few errors and several names overlooked besides some recruits received since who of course did not figure as members of our company. I shall endeavor in a few days to you another list and a correct one for the benefit of the friends of those who have come with us. Some typographical errors were in the list, as for instance the name of Corp. Willi, which is printed D. Gum Willie when it should be David Montgomery Davidson Willi! He requested to have it corrected.

I have also failed to notice our very gentlemanly barber and hairdresser John C. Scott from Lancaster. He is a very accommodating son of Ethiopia, a half-brother of Joe Hawkins, but not half as lazy. Our celebrated pack horse Lemuel Grayson, another dark-browed Abyssinian who so distinguished himself on the march to Bull Run by carrying the baggage of half the company was also neglected. The *amende honorable* having been done to all I will now close by merely remarking that Capt. Stafford is the best tactician in camp, the best fellow in camp, and is liked by everybody in the camp while Lt. Wiley has done his best to learn all he could and at the time put on no snobbish airs, as some do who glory in red tape and embroidered shoulder straps.

Weekly Lancaster Gazette, October 3, 1861, pg. 1

Camp Corwin, Dayton, Ohio
October 16, 1861

Since my last but little of interest has transpired here in camp, but what little I shall communicate to you merely in order to keep up my correspondence till other scenes in a more belligerent clime shall make my epistles interesting if not agreeable.

Brig. Gen. McCook returned one week ago from Washington City whither he had been getting instructions, orders, and commissions, and gave the boys one of the old fashioned three months' drills of about four hours duration on the common, in the sun around the city and at a double quick! He left us next morning for the seat of coming war in Kentucky to take charge of the Buckeye boys in that 'dark and bloody ground.' The commission of colonel of the 1st Ohio has been gerrymandered to Benjamin F. Smith[7] of New Jersey, although our worthy Lt. Col. Edwin A. Parrott would have been the choice of 99 and 32/100s of the non-commissioned officers and privates of our regiment and the unanimous choice of the commissioned officers. Parrott is not a large man in physical proportion but mentally he is a scrounger. His pluck has been thoroughly tested heretofore, as he is the same lieutenant colonel who led Stafford's and Dister's companies on towards Vienna after the inhuman massacre of the advance guard of the 1st Ohio by a masked battery of four guns directed by two South Carolina regiments and made up the covering retreat with the division under his command.

Gen. McCook is still our commander and we leave shortly for the scene of the conflict to join those noble souls from Ohio who will compose McCook's brigade and it may be that we will soon clasp by the hands those who have been our companions in childhood and out intimate friends in maturity. I thank God, although the vote of Fairfield County at the late election, appears to me to be against the cause of truth, justice, and human rights against the best government ever instituted by man against loyalty and in favor of rebellion, against the interests of the North, against the interests of the South, against the interests of the Union and its whole people, very nearly one regiment and a half are now in arms from my native county to do battle for the "Union, the Constitution, and the enforcement of the laws.' It would indeed be a pleasure to meet them in such a state under such circumstances.

No regiment in the United States could be treated better than we have been here by the citizens of Dayton and vicinity, good warm meals when we got to town from almost everybody, lodging if we desire it, picnics gotten up by the ladies almost every day for us, rides when room in the omnibuses to and from the city and in one half day they raised up 950 blankets, some money, overcoats, pieces of carpet, drawers, undershirts, etc. as free and appreciative donations. We are now supplied with sufficient clothing for winter (with the exception of army overcoats) to withstand all the blasts of the Arctic regions.

Our rifled arms have just arrived, the Enfield rifles for the flank companies (A and B) and the Minie rifles for the color and center companies, cartridges, caps, belts, etc. are also here. We have been leaving on tomorrow for a long time, but our departure in my opinion will be speedy. We have battalion drills regularly twice a day and are very well drilled in all the facings, marchings, turns, wheels, flanks, etc. which go to make up the military evolutions of a one third Scott, one third Hardee, and one third Zouave drill. How we will progress in the manual of arms remains to be seen, but as we have many farmer boys among us well drilled with the shot gun, we'll wait for further information.

A and B companies are drilled in the skirmish maneuvers at odd intervals daily and this important branch of military tactics is receiving its appropriate attention.

Us boys from the city proper, unaccustomed to the woodland songsters, get up before the morning reveille to hear the 'little birds sing praises to God.' This early rising was inaugurated in camp by Private. Minor R. Poulton and readily followed by those who can appreciate the stillness of the morning and the beauties of nature. Capt. John Crowe of the first 1st Ohio who is now raising a company for the war hearing of the distinguished correspondent of the *Lancaster Gazette* of my good looks, my intelligence, capacity, and honesty, added to my immense personal bravery tendered to Capt. Stafford my appointment as first lieutenant in his company, but as a 'private at the tail end of the rear rank' of Stafford's company, among our own boys, is good enough for me. I declined the flattering honor.

Among those who have visited us I must mention Mr. and Mrs. Samuel Herr, who were on a visit to relatives in Dayton but called to see us frequently and I have reason to say that their visits were mutually agreeable. Also the visit of John Groff, who the boys will forever remember with feelings of gratitude. The delicacies in the way of food, fried chickens, apple butter, old fashioned pies, fried cakes, dried beef, etc. which are presented to us were very acceptable, but news he brought us from home, the little things he told us which others had forgotten, those small items which letter writers forget and soldiers love to hear were more acceptable, making his home camp among us for a few days, he left with regret to perform his duty at the ballot box by voting the whole Union ticket, all the time showing a deep and soul-felt interest in the justice and magnamity of our cause and a possibility that he has seen for the last time numerous friends and a loved brother.

By the time this is in print, if numerous rumors are true or near it, we will be in another locality, till then, au revoir.

Weekly Lancaster Gazette, October 24, 1861, pg. 1

Camp Yoke near Nashville Depot, Louisville, Kentucky
November 8, 1861

Leaving the Cincinnati barracks after the receipt of a heavy pair of shoes and a splendid new overcoat apiece, and after the condemned French muskets of the center companies had been exchanged for improved Springfield muskets of the patent Greenwood rifling, we embarked aboard the magnificent mail steamboats *Telegraph No. 3* and *Major Anderson* arriving at Louisville about half-past ten at night, the regiment being marched to the Nashville Depot, the staff officers showing their extreme good judgment by selecting Lt. Emanuel T. Hooker as officer and myself as sergeant of the guard, detailed 50 men to act as safe keepers of the baggage, horses, provisions, forage, and equipments of camp.

On our way hither 'down the Ohio' we caught glimpses of Lawrenceburg, Indiana, Aurora, Rising Sun, Patriot, Vevay, and the city of Madison, also the towns of

Ghent, Warsaw, and Carrollton, Kentucky. All along the river a distance of over 150 miles, Union banners were floating in the breeze and waved by people of all ages and both sexes. At Warsaw, a salute was fired by the citizens from one of Uncle Sam's baby wakers which aroused the echoes from the hills and brought forth innumerable cheers from the stout-lunged men of the 1st Ohio. This place a short time since was the headquarters of secession bushwhackers who sneaked around by day, prowled around by night, picking off Union men and stealing from everybody. But the hardy sons of that district, sound to the core, vigorous and active, loving country more than rascally relatives, shouldered their muskets, pocketed their revolvers, and drove them to 'Sweet Owen.'

Arrived in the depot in the city of Louisville, we were furnished with the best breakfast it has been my lot to partake of since our removal towards Kentucky. It is furnished to all regiments passing through the city gratis by the Union Subsistence Committee, kept up by private donations from loyal citizens thus rendering the tax capital of seceshers extremely limited in that regard. I stepped yesterday morning into the editorial room of the *Louisville Journal* and introduced myself as an old typo driven out of curiosity to visit the most eminent man of the tripod. He received me with cordiality and expressed himself always gratified to meet a Union soldier and grasp him by the hand. George D. Prentice [8] is indeed a noble specimen of a whole-souled man. Intellectuality and honesty shine forth from his countenance and although growing old he has neither lost one iota of his zeal for his country or his love of human rights. Gen. William T. Sherman is also here as military dictator. Too laconic for one whose superfluities are largely developed in conversational matters, I did not call on him.

What has become of the saddle and harness makers of Lancaster? Has business slackened, or the shop proprietors failed? We have Spencer Bagley, Bill Ross, and Charley Young with us. At Cincinnati, we saw Silas Jeffries, Joseph Webster, James Walters, and Noah Walters; here we have seen Oliver Stoneburner, Daniel Kiner, Isaac Calendine, and James Keller, the latter one of Stafford's old three months' men who has taken a notion to go with us again.

While I write there is an infernal clatter, the noise and confusion incident to removing to another locality, the breaking up of camp, tearing down, packing up with everybody as bosses. We remove some 60 miles from here towards Bowling Green and in the vicinity of Green River where Gen. McCook's command is posted, and from whence a forward movement is to be made soon. It will be a march of three days' duration, the first of any magnitude that we've had. We go to a part of the country overrun until recently by Gen. Simon B. Buckner and mail facilities are not of a very reliable kind but shall continue to write and wish our friends at home to do the same, both taking chances of receiving.

Weekly Lancaster Gazette, November 14, 1861, pg. 3

In this rare 1861 view of Colonel Alexander McDowell McCook (right) and Lieutenant Colonel Edwin A. Parrott (left) of the original 1st Ohio Infantry, Parrott's diminutive size is readily apparent. Despite being too small to serve as an enlisted man, the former state senator, political opponent of Clement Vallandigham, and personal friend of President Abraham Lincoln was the first man in Ohio to enlist in the Civil War. He was well regarded by his men, Comer describing Parrott as a "regular brick, a soldier true." Parrott led the regiment at Bull Run in 1861, and fought with it at Shiloh, but missed Stones River and later battles while on detached duty as provost marshal in Ohio. Parrott sat upon the platform while Lincoln delivered the Gettysburg Address in 1863 and lived to the ripe age of 100, dying in Princeton, New Jersey on September 20, 1931. (Larry M. Strayer Collection)

Camp Armstrong, Hardin Co., Kentucky
November 14, 1861

We arrived here last Saturday-West Point, Hardin Co., Kentucky is a small village of 15-20 houses and is in itself of little importance, but as a place of strategic import is worthy of observation. It is situated on a point of land where the Salt River empties into the Ohio. It is the only practicable way for the Rebels to reach Louisville in case they whip out the Union forces at Bowling Green. Gen. Sherman has wisely seen to matters in this vicinity and as no sensible and prudent general will plan a battle without seeing an outlet in case of defeat, four regiments of infantry will be constantly here. Above us, stretching out as far as the eye can reach is the already famous Muldraugh's Hill and fortified for miles with trenches, embankments, and parapets. Ten pieces of cannon, rifled and smoothbore, point their dread openings in every direction, commanding the rivers at all points for three or four miles. The regiments now here are the 37th Indiana, 9th Michigan, 18th Ohio, and the 1st Ohio who have been digging trenches, bouldering sand banks, felling trees, and mounting cannon. Say our troops are whipped out at Bowling Green, that our forces are driven from Green River, that Elizabethtown is taken back, here is the only place to retreat through and here is the place where grape, canister and round shot, bombshells, copper balls, muskets, and rifles will prevent the execution of Gen. Buckner's toast that he would 'winter in Louisville and hang George D. Prentice to the highest tree.' There is a five rifle cannon battery on the Indiana side of the river commanded by a German company, either piece of which can be so directed as to hit a two foot tree at a distance of three miles.

Our march from Louisville here was very tedious to many- a distance of 21 miles. We pack when on a march a haversack with provisions, a canteen of water, an extra pair of shoes, two large blankets, drawers and shorts, knapsack, 20 rounds of cartridges, cartridge box, a heavy overcoat, besides our rifles and rest about every four miles. Two distressing accidents have happened at this camp. The first was the accidental discharge of a carbine by a cavalryman from Indiana which took effect in the side of one of his comrades, causing a severe wound. The other was the igniting through carelessness of a lot of blank cartridges which communicated to the ball cartridges, blew up a tent, and everything consumable in the tent was speedily in flames. Two of the three men injured may not recover, the other is doing well and is about. The two first are Sergeant Charles Wherrett and Sergeant Henry W. Galloway, the latter Private William Duncan, all of Company D, the Cleveland Grays. Galloway and Wherrett have the skin burned and scorched all over, the finger nails peeled off, while neither have the ability to open their eyes. I have just been in the hospital to see them and I do not wish to see them again under the circumstances. Wherrett and Duncan were acquaintances of mine in the three months' campaigning in eastern Virginia.[9]

Night before last our sentinels were fired upon by about a half dozen unfriendly assailants at as many different points. The long roll was beaten, the battalion formed, and Company A sent out to scour the woods as skirmishers and after all sorts of maneuvers over three or four miles, returned towards camp where the entire regiment was under arms. We retired to rest but three different times afterwards during the night, we were aroused from coveted slumber to arms, but the bushwhackers, satisfied for the night, molested us no more. To the credit of Capt. Stafford's company, be it said that 90 men went on the skirmish in the woods, through briars and up to their knees in mud holes and prairies. Ninety men out of 98 when ten should have been on guard at camp was tolerably good turnout!

Last night we were out on picket guard and it was a novel position for many. Our position was taken in the Muldraugh Hill hollow, where mountains seemed to be piled on mountains, on the top of which, to use the very expressive language of one of our boys, 'you have to stoop to hear it thunder.' We saw nothing but a bearer of dispatches to our temporary brigade, one mountain cat, two turkey gobblers supposed to be wild, some bushes shaking, several large snakes, and several scared boys. We are now under marching order again, all being anxious to get to McCook. Our regiment was raised up by him; we have all along supposed we were to be in his brigade, but the most strenuous exertions have been made to place us in other hands. Every private and all the officers with possibly the exception of Col. B.F. Smith want to be with Ohio's general and the dispatches last night from him gave rise to enthusiasm and imparted new life to the men, giving as they did, the information that the '1st Ohio is not to be brigaded; I raised it up and am going to have it with me; I want no more shillamahoying.'

P.S. Couldn't some of my old chums and acquaintances or some of my many sweethearts write me a letter or two enclosing a postage stamp? Capt. Stafford gave me this paper, Lt. Hooker loaned me the pen, Lt. Wiley the ink, Sgt. Homan the board to write on, Jack Reed the envelope, Charley Young the wafer, and I stole the postage stamp myself.

Weekly Lancaster Gazette, November 21, 1861, pg. 3

Camp Nevin, Hardin Co., Kentucky
November 21, 1861

Taking up our line of march from West Point, a distance of 36 miles from here, we made, in conjunction with the 18th Ohio and 37th Indiana, a tramp of 17 miles on Friday last when we encamped upon an open plain in swamp land where a striking contrast was presented to the rough, hilly, and broken land through which we had that day been passing. A 4 o'clock next morning, the reveille was sounded, an apology for breakfast gotten up, horses hitched, and wagons and temporary brigade gotten under way, and after an up-and-down-side step-oblique journey of 19 miles more, arrived here, passing many a deserted house by the way, seeing nothing but grinning darkies and superannuated white men, with once and a while a woman dressed in black. We passed through Elizabethtown, 10 miles from here, where Buckner put his men on the cars in the time of his advance in the night towards Louisville and where he dumped them off when on his retreat back. Here the 9th Illinois was stationed as railroad guard and the 37th Indiana with the 18th Ohio dropped from our caravan to do likewise.

Such a country as we passed through as regards spontaneous productions one does not often see. Sarvisberries, thumac, blackhaws, tarpahoes, persimmons, apples, turnips, wild grapes, onions, etc. literally lined the road for over 20 miles of the journey, and the member of Capt. Stafford's company who were in the advance guard the first day improved their time to the benefit of the Commissary Department. Two miles this side of Elizabethtown and eight miles from where we are now, we were ordered to 'Battalion! Halt! Front! Right Dress! Present arms!' Who should be coming down the line but General McCook! Guns were thrown down, caps flung in the air, wagons halted, while such a score of wild hurrahs rent the air as was never before heard in that possum hollow! He was surrounded by his bodyguard (dressed in grayish green) and looked as smiling and buoyant as a Dutch boy going to a kraut dinner. Shaking hands with hundreds he went on his way to town, promising to join us in a half hour after our arrival. Everybody was pleased to see him and I know he was pleased to see us, as every motion testified.

We are kept here as a guard to the general's headquarters and one company is detailed per day for that duty. We are in no brigade and under no one's orders but Gen. McCook. You can look which way you please and you will find regiments dotted in, around and about you. Here are Pennsylvania regiments, Michigan, Wisconsin, Illinois, Indiana, Kentucky, and Ohio and it is impossible for anyone not having facts and figures to give a approximate guess of numbers. I can say, however, without magnifying that at least 30 regiments of Union troops are within a radius of 10 miles, some of the excellently drilled. The German regiment of Col. Willich (32nd Indiana) in particular does admirably. Col. Willich has seen service in the Hungarian and Prussian wars, gives his commands in German, and as soldiers of the Fatherland are taught in infancy the principle of the soldier- obedience- they present a striking contrast to the bummers and do-as-you-please of other regiments.

The Rousseau Brigade of Kentuckians is about one mile in rear of us. General Johnston's command in front. The latter brigade contains four regiments, an Illinois, and Indiana, and two Ohio- the 15th and 49th. These two, with the 1st and the 18th, are the only Ohio regiments I have seen outside of cavalry and artillery. The 15th was raised up at Mansfield, Ohio; the 18th in Congressman Horton's stronghold- Athens, Vinton, and Meigs counties. The 49th was raised at Tiffin and is commanded by Col. William H. Gibson, former Treasurer of State, who still uses his choice rhetoric and oratorical powers in speechmaking. The subject- the best way to kill Secesh!

General William T. Sherman, better known as 'Cump Sherman' is Major General of the forces in Kentucky and honored us with a visit and review on Sunday, but the boys of our company, those of advanced age, were not recognized by him, although a former playmate, born in the same place, and still bound to the old home by kindred and social ties. Loquacity is detected by him; conversation, except on business, strictly forbidden; at the same time, to meet him off duty is to meet a genial, communicative companion- a whole-souled intellectual officer and man.

We occasionally hear of the 17th but can't get its precise location. Sometimes it is 100 miles off, at others times varying from 25 up; if we meet, there will be such a reunion as will make the angels in heaven shed tears for joy. We have received no pay yet but have plenty to eat and wear. Privates, corporals, and sergeants are about dead broke, and most of the captains and lieutenants have spent their last flint sometime since and have to pay their own expenses besides. Poor fellows. 'I told them not to come.'

One of our boys got a letter from home which stated that a box of provisions were to be sent to us; likewise some woolen stockings. Don't send any provisions but good, old-fashioned country stockings, all wool knit in good old Fairfield, sent by way of Louisville, wouldn't be refused. Oh no, a forward movement soon.

Weekly Lancaster Gazette, November 28, 1861, pg. 3

Camp Nevin, Hardin Co., Kentucky
November 26, 1861

Nothing going on here but the general observance and execution of Army regulations such as guard mounting, drilling, etc. and I have only to relate a few incidents of our trip hither coupled with biographical sketches and pen portraits. On our way here, we crossed the famous bridge over Rolling Fork. A half mile above us, leaning on her staff, fording the stream was a negro wench. Starting pursuit, the lieutenant tried to Hook-her but the contraband was wily and copying him cried out "Ho!Man! you can't come it, you haven't got your Holtzman!' To all appearances, she was young, her dressed ruffled, her hair knotty, evident needing a 'Comb-er,' she ran so fast they got her knot and here this subject leave I.

The corps were not dead by any means, but Joe-vial, seeing many curious sights. Here a hazel bush or hairy Reed, there a persimmon fence or Applegate, a moving Bill to ope and Shutt, hollows where Old Sol never shown and which soldiers possibly Will-lie. Notwithstanding scenery, they were compelled to Bob around, and whether major or Minor, forced to Pout-on! The privates, Allen-like, As-Bell's tingled for Kentucky dinners, looked for soup Bowles, but saw nothing but barren Bowers; nature's pantries with no Lard-in, our Baker was of no account, our Porter uncometable, our Murphys none the best, fresh meat all consumed, and though we often saw a live Wolfe and wanted to Schute our Cap, who fitted nice and could Call-well, kept us in ranks and no Arcadian castle, however inviting, gave us a Heist. We were compelled to grin and Barrett. We at length got here, where no civil Law reaches; Autumn has put on her Brown, the leaves are Frizelled, the winter birds Carrell sadly; Bis singer warbles his beauteous strains; Stutzman in his Dennis, a smooth face is as good as a Harriman; the order now is- Coff man and eject you Flemm, the water in the pond is Riley, the highways Rockey, while swamp land makes good Myers. Our Wagner has been Shook and others will soon get an ague Webb wove around them. All this are Horney, but no Railer however good a Mauler, or Carpenter, or Mason, or Smith, or Hunters for pleasure could do Moore than us to secure comfort, keep our quarters clean, and our rifles without a speck or Dent-on. We leave here shortly to clean out Buckner, take in Zollicoffer and then with the aid of Spencer, Bagg-Lee! The firm of Peter, Sons, and Co. has gone to Cleveland. A little boat, the Odore, under command of an experienced Sailor, the weather without a Cloud or Speck carried them safely over the billowy Rhodes.

Having gone through this immense strain upon my mental powers, I will now picture you various notables in this locality. Col. B.F. Smith is a native of New Jersey and a relative of Gov. Dennison. He is a man about 5 feet 9 inches in height, light, sallow complexion, a regular graduate of West Point where enjoyed the privileges at one time of a lieutenant in the regular army. Latterly, he was employed by the Chicago Air Line Railroad Company from which position he was transplanted to the colonelcy of the 1st Ohio which adorns him very well. Lt. Col. Edwin A. Parrott is a person exceedingly small in stature, being below the height required for a soldier in the ranks. He is a native of Dayton, Ohio where he was the prominent political opposer of whatever Vallandigham has said or done. He is a tried soldier, served at Fall's Church and Bull Run as lieutenant colonel of the three months' troops and now occupies the same position with the entire confidence of the regiment. He was formerly President of the Senate, pro. tem. of Ohio. Major E. Bassett Langdon is a man of Herculean proportions, 6 feet 4 inches high, and weighted accordingly. He, too, was a former member of our state legislature and acted in the capacity of the Speaker of the House of Representatives during two successive Democratic state administrations. He is a Jacksonian in will but too phlegmatic in action. His home is in Cincinnati.

Our sutlers, Jake Starling of Cincinnati and Jim Collier of Steubenville are the personages that 'draw crowded houses.' Each soldier is allowed a credit of $5.50 per month. A description of the contour of these two may not be uninteresting. Jake is a crane-looking individual 7 feet 9 inches high, weighing over 100 pounds, well-liked by everybody and always willing to do one a favor. Jim is nearly the opposite of Jake physically. Imagine one of Younghan's big beer hogsheads multiplied by two and you have the corposity of Jim; his neck is built in proportion, his legs encased in immaculate unmentionables are about 11 inches long, supported by feet something near the length of Jake's leg. He, too, is always willing to do a favor- when it pays him.

Company A is a bright particular star which still draws round, as if by magnetic influence the members of other companies. A jolly captain, gay lieutenants, and a bully crew, stoves in several tents, good fellows in all of them, and the log cabin tent built by the labor of the company for the captain and his staff and the sutler's establishment between the company tents and the log cabin make our situation most prominent, but at the same time subjects us to blame for all the noise created in the right wing direction and the suspicion is likewise created that various articles missed by our vending functionary have by some means or the other found a habitation in Company A's haversacks and knapsacks!

Weekly Lancaster Gazette, December 12, 1861, pg. 3

Jim Collier and Jake Starling (Abby Kitcher)

Camp en route, Kentucky
December 10, 1861

Sunday last we got marching orders at Camp Nevin and yesterday (Tuesday) started. A quantity of baggage with the sick and disabled and a few guards was sent to McCook's station, a distance of two miles; those being so severely sick as to be in hospital having previously been sent to the army hospital at Louisville. Owing to natural ruggedness and cleanliness, the 1st Ohio sent far fewer sick away than any other regiment. Two of Company A's boys were sent- John F. Barrett and John Heberly. Barrett has been sick for some time but until lately Heberly has been one of the stoutest and heartiest fellows in camp; a severe fever took hold of him lately and it was thought best to remove him where he could recover more speedily than in camp. All the others are alive and kicking, full of fun, frolic, fire, and fuss-fat, ragged, sassy, good-natured, and big eaters!

The boys that marched here yesterday say the road was muddy most all the time, although the occasionally came across places where it was not much over shoe deep. I was one of the fortunate individuals who contrived to make the surgeon believe they had a bellyache and got a railroad ride with the sick and baggage, and know nothing personally of the roads, but from muddy shoes, muddy trousers, muddy shirts, muddy coats, muddy caps, muddy haversacks, muddy faces and muddy knapsacks, other regiments besides the 17th can get in mud and march over bad roads. At least fifteen regiments went through the same as us, as many more were passed, and there was about one brigade in advance of us when we all arrived here.

Two brigades, neither containing less than three regiments, have passed on this morning to Green River, a distance of ten miles where they halt, then 'we, us, and company' marching the same route tomorrow pass them and all taking up our line of march will by some means or the other cross the river and be within the sacred limits of General Buckner's Secessia- not exactly where the future mincemeat of the Union troops are quartered, but in a country they claim as their own and which they have sworn shall never be polluted by the 'mercenary hirelings, ruthless invaders, abolition mobs, Negro lovers, merciless marauders, Hessians, and Lincoln thieves' but all the expletives and adjectives used by the classic gentlemen of Palmettodom to designate Union forces will avail them nothing, and in due course of time, will come home to roost.

At present writing in sight is the terminus of the Louisville & Nashville railroad. How it came to terminate here is in this way: right along this neck of the woods is the little village of Wasp's Nest, which beautiful nomenclature was given to it by a gang of gamblers and horse thieves who made it their headquarters until the breaking out of the war, since which time that have enlisted in the cause of Southern rights! The Louisville and Nashville Railroad passes through the nest but the Secesh still left in around and about the place are never satisfied unless the large railroad bridge over Bacon Creek is down, fearing the transportation of men and supplies by the United States. With this end in view, they have burned it down three times in the past two months, the last time four days ago. The bridge will be speedily rebuilt and a force sufficient to protect it left here.

Yesterday I witnessed the taking to the burial ground of a member of a Pennsylvania regiment. A rude, rough coffin made with scanty material yet showing care contained all that was left of one who had gone to peril his life for his country. He was buried with Christian formality and by kind and sorrowing companions; but it must indeed be hard for a soldier to die away from home, in the midst of war, without getting to strike one blow for the cause of Union. Gen. Buckner on last Saturday sent 20 men and a captain with a flag of truce to Gen. McCook asking permission to send the dead body of his son to Louisville for interment, which was granted. If we move tomorrow, good; if we don't, the dickens take the delay.

Weekly Lancaster Gazette, December 19, 1861, pg. 3

Camp Wood, Green River, Kentucky
December 22, 1861

I have been troubled with that bane of any climate-chills and fever- for six days up to Thursday last, since which time I have been watching the results of numerous doses of calomel, quinine, salts, and rhubarb I have taken. I have now no complaint but a slight cough, yet I am still weak. This will account for my not writing you lately; also for not answering several letters I have received from Fairfield.

Tuesday last, the entire force at Bacon Creek was moved here- Johnson's Brigade being here in advance. Rousseau's Brigade (the one to which we are attached), Wood's, Negley's, and a regiment of cavalry with about six full batteries is the force now here. In the camp we left, other brigades have come to since, but will not be moved until the completion of the railroad bridge over the Green River, as it would be utter folly to advance troops in an enemy's country without having adequate means of transportation for army supplies which must follow.

The bridge which the Rebels tried to blow up here is the most superb work of the kind I have ever seen. It is 800 feet long (or ought to be), built entirely of iron, and supported by fours piers with two stone abutments running from the water up a distance of 80 feet. A company of laborers have agreed to reconstruct it so far as to answer the purpose of travel in eight days (about four yet) when the heavy advance may be expected, but there is no telling how far we advance, for the same fell spirit that attempted the destruction of such a magnificent work as the Green River railroad bridge has undoubtedly torn up track and despoiled other bridges.

I should have mentioned before this that the day of our arrival here, the 32nd Indiana commanded by Col. Willich was attacked by a force of Texas Rangers and Rebel cavalry estimated variously at 800-2,500 troopers. The men who were engaged in the fight on our sides, all Germans, behaved manfully and heroically and contested the unequal fight with cool bravery and dauntless daring. Eighty-five of the Rebels are reported killed by those of the enemy who returned to the battlefield under a flag of truce, among them Col. Terry and Capt. Pfeiffer. Several magnificent horses, better drilled than a great many men I know of, were taken by our men and several double barreled shotguns. The saddle and bridles on the horses were of the regular Texas pattern- the bridles of mixed hair, platted, the stirrups of wood covered with leather, with high stout horn to saddle. On the other hand, our loss was considerably smaller, but eleven new made graves fifty yards from our quarters, two who have been sent home for interment, and 20 wounded in the hospital attest but too plainly a devotion to freedom's cause not commensurate with prudence.[10]

Reports came into camp from scouts on Wednesday night 12 o'clock that General Thomas C. Hindman of Arkansas had advanced 4,000 troops by rail to within three miles of us. Before daylight, a full brigade of United States men had crossed the river and planted their batteries. There were thrown out as pickets, the 1st Ohio among them, who stood on the lookout in line until relieved on Friday by another brigade. Saturday the 14th was payday and was received with general rejoicing. $29.90 was the amount received by the men, being their pay for 2 months 9 days, the greater portion of which was sent home, each taking his own way of dispatching it on account of Mr. N. Young not coming as anticipated.

Nothing more now, but another letter soon.

Weekly Lancaster Gazette, January 2, 1862, pg. 1

Camp Wood, north bank of Green River, Hart Co., Kentucky
December 29, 1861

'Tis seldom one can well rehearse
Events in camp with neat strung verse,
But surely 'tis no harm to try,
One's hand sometimes. Here goes though I,
May not keep time, or always meter,
I'll speak the truth; that's something sweeter.

You've heard no doubt, 'mong papers old,
Of B.F. Smith, our Colonel bold,
Whose splendid form and manly grace,
Whose huge mustache and buoyant face,
Stentorian voice, majestic stride,
Has given the 1st a fame world wide.

Not for battle bravely won,
Not for val'rous deeds we've done,
But for our tact and precious skill,
In shirking duty, skipping drill,
Marching roughly, finding pickins',

Such as roosts and little chickens!

We also know a thing or two,
'Bout drills battalion, we can do.
Our work up quick, if not quite true-
Enough to suit such prying eyes,
As those thro' which McClellan spies,
Potomac's army, let this suffice.

Lieutenant Colonel Parrott, four foot two,
(A regular brick, a soldier true),
Who at Bull Run would run'd it stronger,
If legs had been a little longer,
Sits on a horse, a second Hummel,
Almost as high as saddle's pummel!

There's Major Langdon, six feet four,
At least, if needed, something more,
Who watches 'biz' with careful eye,
And officers who wish to try,
A shirk of duty, oft get fooled,
And in court martial get well schooled.

Adjutant Parrott needs no joggin',
He's got the tactics in his noggin.
He bellows well, turns fair and square,
Upon his heel, la militaire.
Then goes to bed upon his couch,
And dreams till morn or Rodepouch!

We're right across from Woodsonville,
A little town upon a hill,
Green River goes a surging by,
And oftentimes, its strength does try,
Against the bridge the Dutch have made,
To keep our army from a wade!

Our boys are well and rations good,
In fact we've got quite handsome food.
We drill with knapsacks twice a day,
But that's a thing that don't quite pay,

Our tents are good, well put together,
And only leak in rainy weather!

Our surgeon makes a daily round,
To see if sickness can be found,
If any's found, woe to the man,
Whose optic vision has to scan,
Take and digest, without recoil,
The quarts of salts and castor oil!

We leave next year for Bowling Green,
Too see the sights and to be seen,
If anything turns up, I'll write,
Before that time, till then, good night.

Please send a paper, do not tarry,
Your correspondent,
Handsome Harry

Weekly Lancaster Gazette, January 9, 1862, pg. 1

Camp Wood, north bank of Green River, Hart Co., Kentucky
January 1, 1862

Today like Christmas was spent by the 1st Ohio on outpost picket duty across Green River, the reserve occupying the ground of the late skirmish between the Texas Rangers and Col. Willich's German regiment. Nothing was seen of the rebellious foe, and we returned to camp this evening tired, sleepy, hungry, wet and dry! No beauteous vision met our eyes of neat and clean table cloth, no warm biscuits or tea sent the hot blood through our veins, no nice and flavory turkey with the seasoned dressing met us with tempting look to depart down the great gateway of fat pork, pilot crackers, and dishwater coffee. Our New Year and Christmas festivities were indeed unlike yours but we had our rough sports still. The whole world seems convulsed by war, and the law of love is displaced in our land by the madness of civil strife.

But there is a silver lining to the portentous cloud and it is most truthfully portrayed by a writer in the *New York Post* who says "how many families with gather around the domestic hearth with kindliness, the sympathy, the sweet exchange of affection, and the joy which the season prompts, and yet with a low undertone of bereaved and wounded feeling? The little children will laugh and clap their hands over their gifts, but many of them will miss the complacent paternal countenance which beamed in sunshine over all the group; the tender and busy wife will smile on their innocent satisfaction but momentarily drop tears for one that is not by; the cheery friend, the welcome guest, will not find his wonted seat. Many a brother, many a son-for the first time, perhaps- will take no part in the gambols of the other sisters and brothers making vain pretense of gladness with an awful sense of some mute shadows watching all. Alas! They will be far away where the dear sweet scenes of home will only be a remembrance; some sleeping on earth beneath the raw winds and cold rains of winter, some alone and dismal on the distant midnight outposts, others perhaps tossing in the tumult of battle while the whole air throbs with volleys of cannon or writhing in the throes of death, or gone from the light forever. Yet these painful experiences will be relieved by a consoling and comforting consciousness. No one who suffers or dies for his county, for honor, for justice, for truth, for liberty, suffers or dies in vain."

None of Company A are sick with the exception of our very worthy and well beloved captain. It is now nearly three weeks since he was taken down with bilious fever. He is now gaining health and strength daily, and the brigade surgeon promises for him a speedy recovery. His company have felt his non-appearance among them very much, and from the solicitude expressed for his welfare by all that know him, the 1st Ohio also. The physician has advised him to go home a couple of weeks to recruit his strength, but 'Captain Joe' like a true man and soldier as he undoubtedly is, says he wants no furlough and Company A is a good enough home for him. After he has been sick for about a week, the boys, unbeknownst to him, sent to Louisville for a nice sword, tassel, and accoutrements, which were presented to him by your humble servant on behalf of the company. He accepted the present with heartfelt emotion and weak as he was, poured out his thanks in vivid and impassioned eloquence, not studied, but coming from the innermost depths of the soul like the gushing up of a spring in the mountains.

Last Saturday December 28, a beautiful flag was presented by Gen. James S. Negley's brigade to Gen. Lovell H. Rousseau's, composed of the 5th Kentucky (Louisville Legion), one regiment of regulars, the 6th Indiana, and the 1st Ohio. The presentation speech was made fittingly by George D. Prentice of the *Louisville Journal* in a happy and yet solemn speech of great power and vivid imagination; and responded to in a patriotic, logical, well-timed, eloquent, and powerful speech from Brig. Gen. Rousseau. Surrounded by thousands of talented men in regulation uniform and bayonets glistening in the winter sun, it was no wonder Prentice said that "this is an event which time or place shall never efface from my memory."

Since writing you last, two of our regiment have stepped the narrow abyss of time and their souls been launched into a never ending eternity; they were buried in the honors of war and although no unfriendly bullet made their life blood flow, they nevertheless fell in the cause of justice and humanity, a prey to camp malaria, dampness, and inadequate medical attendance. Rest in peace brave comrades, a crown of glory in heaven is yours.

That model of architectural skill and science-the Green River bridge of the Louisville and Nashville railroad is not yet reconstructed, but a few days more and the iron horse will go snorting on his way to Secessia, drawing in his train all sorts of army supplies. For temporary purposes a footbridge capable of bearing up unloaded wagons has been constructed. Lately however, a pontoon bridge, the finest and most perfect of any I have yet seen has been made. A pontoon is made in a sort of half canoe, half scow manner placed parallel with the running water, tightened together, and planked over. Tightened in place by ropes, it is always in its right place, rising and falling as the depth of water dictates. After answering the purposes of crossing a stream, the pontoons can be taken up and used as wagon beds.

It is astonishing how many old friends who had never expected to see each other again meet together in war times. I have seen acquaintances from Minnesota, Michigan, Iowa, Illinois, Indiana, and Pennsylvania. Here I have met the Abrams of Illinois, Fahnestock's, Williams', Jim Neibling, Dock Shaw, Dan Richards, Frank Durbin, Soc Lydy, Ike Wyman, and scores of others formerly from our county but now gathered in from all points to share in the dangers, fatigues, and glory of a battle for the Union. I shall not bore you again with a letter until something of at least slight importance turns up, but will end with the sly hint that Company A, 1st Ohio Volunteers would not feel in the least offended if a box of tobacco and provisions was sent to Capt. Stafford's company as a New Year's present. Rumor has it that about 60,000 Rebels, armed to the teeth and backed by good artillery, are waiting for us at Bowling Green and intend demolishing the whole of the Union Lincolnites. If I am to be killed, let me die with a full stomach of Fairfield County grub!

Weekly Lancaster Gazette, January 9, 1862, pg. 3

Camp Wood, Green River, Kentucky
January 12, 1862

The bridge, so notorious lately, situated across the crossing over Green River, is at length completed. Thanks to good weather, stout arms, mechanical ingenuity, willing hearts, and Providence. It is not as beautiful or magnificent as it should be or once was, but there it stands, stretching out over 800 feet in length, nigh 100 feet above water, half trestle work, half iron- a symbol of the fell spirit of Southern laziness and destructiveness, and a monument to the self-reliant labor of freemen raised under free institutions, relying on their own good right arms. A rifle pit is being dug over the river, in which two regiments left to guard the bridge can find cover in case another attempt to blow it up, being made by superior forces, and an advance or removal from our present situation may confidently be expected, but how soon? There's the rub. General Buell's dispatches to me are very unsatisfactory.

On Thursday last, Capt. Stafford left for home to recruit his strength, every vestige of fever having left him. I presume he arrived home safely, as his old employee Lem Prayson of Culpepper Co., Virginia accompanied him. He had lain sick for about three weeks, but his departure for home cast a funeral spell over his company which, up to this time, had not been entirely dissipated. The fact is that he is the best loved man in the 1st Ohio and likes his men in return. A shoulder strap and bars don't make him lose his kindness of heart or gentlemanly bearing.

Furloughs are being made out for three of our boys to go home on sick list, but as several officials have undergone court martial trials for doing business up with too much alacrity, those who have the health and comfort of the men in charge don't wish to run the same risk, and therefore, delay, delay, delay when two weeks home care would bring the boys back to health and happiness.

Out on picket the other day with the 30th Indiana, most of us were agreeably surprised to find a tall, bearded, soldier-looking captain. Joseph Braden, Esq., formerly superintendent of the Fairfield County Infirmary, sporting his sword as vigorously as he once did the birchen rod.

The death and burial accounts of Jacob Lehman fell like a thunderbolt on the heads of those who have been intimate with him from childhood up, knowing him as an intelligent, upright, and conscientious young man, kind and just to all alike, thus cut off in the prime of life and in the heat of his youthful zeal.

There being little or no news to write you at this particular time, I shall content myself by giving you the topography of this neck of woods as it will doubtless before long be the scene of mighty events, a desperate fought battle or an inglorious retreat by the Rebels. The situation I give is partly from scouts, but mostly from a rather unsatisfactory outline map picked up on the bloody grounds of Willich's field of Mars. Behind us, Louisville with her home guard and Buell's reserve; Muldraugh Hill, mouth of Salt River with her fortifications, batteries, and infantry; Nevin with her camps of drilling soldiers; Bacon Creek, with Mitchell's division; us, ourselves here; Munfordville, Woodsonville, Green River, or what you please call it with our 15-20,000 men, infantry, our field artillery, our dragoons and native scouts. In front now 12 miles below us, Gen. Hindman's Rebel advance at Cave City, the celebrated Mammoth Cave; right oblique from there a distance of 23 miles by rail to Bowling Green, strongly fortified with rifle pits, embankments, trenches, masked batteries, behind which I calculate are at least 45,000 men with every conceivable kind of weapon. My estimate is made this way: Buckner's original force which he threatened Louisville was about 20,000; reinforcements by Johnston, 12,000, Breckinridge, 8,000, Floyd, 7,000. It will take time, patience, head work, and nerve to unlodge them as they count three fourths our number, have torn up railroad track, burnt bridges, mined roads and passes, felled trees over roads, planted masked batteries, despoiled the country through which the Union army has to pass, and done all other acts calculated to retard the progress of the law enforcers. With the young and glorious acting major general of our division, A. McD. McCook to counsel by advice and enthuse by presence, we have no fear rushing into ambuscade or exposing ourselves unnecessarily to masked batteries. Next to God and health, we trust in McCook.

Weekly Lancaster Gazette, January 23, 1862, pg. 1

Camp Wood, Hart Co., Kentucky
January 18, 1862

'Now is the winter of our discontent' I ejaculated as I hustled out to roll call on last Thursday morning. The ground was covered with the snowy flakes, huge icicles drooped from the tent flies, the running water of the day before was converted into a crystalline congealment, and the large oaks stood like bony arms of ice as if to clench the passer-by. The cold wind whistled through the branches and went through our sieve-like coats with a screeching scream; and then went sighing down the river as if loathe to leave us. An order goes from headquarters to captains- 'First Ohio for outpost duty today!' We went, of course, for the 1st is always ready to do its duty- when they have no other alternative and in due course of time, we were transferred to the outer picket line, built three separate fires, but were moved from place to place until we arrived where it was neither safe nor prudent to have lights, where we stood until 4 o'clock Friday afternoon. All this time it was pouring down umbrageous clunks of snow and sleet which, just as we started for camp, turned to rain which up to this time has not ceased hostilities. This, however, is but the natural sequence of war; but even in this case, our spirits raised shortly after getting home. A huge store box, filled with 735 pounds of provisions, made its welcome appearance amongst us, sent to mess No. 1 but in which were packages for other messes.

May the Lord bless and prosper those mammies, daddies, sisters, brothers, sugar lumps, and friends who sent the welcome gift; may John Jackson and Nobe Robinson, who superintended the getting up and likewise donated liberally, 'live forever then die happy!' I also hope that the poor boys of our mess who are now suffering from a bellyache may speedily recover and regain their appetites before the healthy boys consume the balance. Hard crackers, fat pork, and semi-occasionally, beans have been our eatables lately; now they are supplanted by fresh sausage, bologna, pudding, cheese, sweitzercase, bread, buns, crullers, sweet cake, gingerbread, pound cake, pies of all kinds, pickles, oysters, chicken, turkey, preserves, plums, cherries, peaches, tobacco, cigars, cherry bounce, catsup, pepper sauce, and 'here's to you!' In this connection, I must not forget to acknowledge for the recipient, a present of a nice brickbat, cut in three slices, from John Noble Robinson, Esquire, which, as our men had enough without, was thrown outside the tent so that others, less favored than us, might have something, too!

Yesterday, we had a big scare in, around, and about here. Two regiments had been sent out on either side of the railroad a distance of two or three miles as scouts. Espying each other and each supposing they were the only Union troops that far out, dispatched messengers to camp in advance and then came themselves at rather more than common time. In 10 minutes, the whole division was in commotion. The different brigades formed and all but the Rousseau Brigade, to which we belong, marched across the river. Instead of it being a large army coming to attack us with a regiment as skirmishers, the fact was soon ascertained and the hoaxed returned sorrowfully to camp- sorry because there was no fight; sorry because their whole bodies were covered in mud.

There is no doubt but what the Rebels see the importance of getting out of their present quarters before they can't and may make a desperate dash to get to Louisville through this route and it behooves us to be watchful. The bridge is guarded all the time and on the south side, trenches, rifle pits, embankments, logs, etc. have been arranged so as to make it possible for 2,000 men to repel an assault of at least double numbers. Writing this merely as an acknowledgement to those who sent us the eatables, that we have received them, I now close with the remark that the *Gazette* didn't send anything.

Weekly Lancaster Gazette, January 30, 1862, pg. 1

Camp Wood, Hart Co., Kentucky
January 31, 1862

It is a very good adage of which I am informed old prosaic but philosophical Ben Franklin was the author that 'when you have nothing to say, say nothing.' But relying firmly on his ability to make as much out of nothing as anyone else and my own imaginative properties, I'll write you once again on the subject of nothing.

The mud is not quite so deep as it was owing to the fact that the sun made its appearance for about two hours and a quarter last Tuesday and the ground freezing this morning to make up for lost time, however, old Father Aquarius has again opened out and as it always pours down in torrents in this country when a rain only has been promised, we may confidently expect to obtain and regain our regular supply of mud. Capt. Stafford arrived at home on last Monday in company with his Lemuel and was greeted by all as the returning prodigal. He looks exceedingly well for the short space of time he has been absent, but there is still about 30 pounds of the original Joe lacking to fill up his clothes to the Jenkenish standard. Lt. James M. Wiley has been detailed from our company to act as assistant division quartermaster and reported himself to Louisville today. From his stability of character, stern integrity, business energy, and long mercantile experience, I am compelled to admit that the appointing power has made a mistake and at length appointed one officer who will understand his duty. Jim's rank and pay will now be that of a captain.

William Cloud, who was from Pleasantville, Fairfield County and first a member of the Lancaster company but afterwards transferred on account of a surplus of numbers to Company D (Cleveland) has paid the debt of nature- dying of measles in the hospital across the river.[11] James Colwell, a member of our company whose parents reside in or near New Holland, Pickaway County also died this morning of the same disease- the first death in Capt. Stafford's companies since the war began.[12] They were both good soldiers and well-liked by their comrades. Let them rest in peace above and may the God of battles and disease grant that the medical department look more to the sick soldier's comfort and recovery than to its own convenience. Let them know and feel that a private soldier has loving friends and family ties as well as an epauletted numb skull. Five more of our company are across the river in hospitals, but are now convalescent and will soon gladden us with their presence: Christopher F. Smith, William

Harvey, William Carlis, Caleb Copeland, Isaac Mason; three in our regimental hospital: Jacob Shook, Eli Stoneburner, and Sgt. John Reese Holtzman. The first five have had the measles, the latter three fever. The rest are in excellent health and considering the perpetual rain we have had for three weeks (with the aforementioned two and quarter hour's sunshine) in first rate spirits.

The 32nd Indiana regiment (German) went on a scout a short time since as far as Cave City, but saw nothing worthy of being taken in out of the damp as the Confederates had confederated together and stole everything they could lay their hands on and then vamoosed for another locality. Not even a cackling hen could be seen and the old agrarian farmers who wait till the cock crows in the morning before they get up out of bed would sleep in this country until Gabriel blew his trumpet. Speaking of Gabriel and his trumpet remains me of a witty assertion made by of Co. A's sharpers. "Floyd stole all the government guns, Buckner stole all the chickens in Hart County, and if the angel Gabriel would come down from heaven to blow his trumpet, the Texas Rangers would steal his instrument before he could sound the first toot!"

Last night, 'Old Zolli' and Bailie Peyton, or rather their dead bodies, arrived in Camp Wood in an embalmed state. They were overnight at McCook's headquarters from whence they were taken under a flag of truce to the Rebel government having requested the "Northern barbarians" to confer an especial favor by doing so. It was an act of magnamity, and in striking contrast to the insulting refusals of the Rebels to us on similar occasions such as in the case of Col. Cameron at Bull Run. [13]

I have several very good reasons for not telling you when we shall advance, but the most potent of all is that I don't know. "I would if I could, if I couldn't how would I? Could I? Could you?" Having succeeded to my own satisfaction in making a silken pecuniary receptacle out of a female bovine's auricular organ- a silk purse out of a sow's ear-much out of nothing-used the ideal where the reality was lacking. I close promising as I always do that if something turns up for Macawber, Macawber will surely write.

P.S. I am still able to eat all my rations.

P.S.S. Most of the company ditto.

P.S.S.S. I always have rheumatism at drill time and get excused from duty!

P.S.S.S.S. None of our company have the itch!

Weekly Lancaster Gazette, February 6, 1862, pg. 3

Chapter Three

SHILOH, CORINTH, AND THE SUMMER OF 1862

Camp Andy Johnson, near Nashville, Tennessee
March 12, 1862

After a long postponement of writing to you on account of tramps, bivouacking, disarranged postal communication, and inadequate mail facilities, I once more have time and opportunity to address you. Friday February 13, McCook's division having received orders to march from Louisville and from thence by boats to where the battle of Fort Donelson was fought started but after a march of 15 miles, the order was countermanded and the order to march back given, the division arriving at their old quarters on Sunday morning, taking up their march in the rear of Gen. Mitchel's division on Monday en route for Bowling Green.

After passing what was left of the Rowlett railroad station, there was not a quarter mile of whole track from that place to Bowling Green-brush and fence rails has been fired on the track and warped the ties and iron rails. Every building capable of being used as a hospital had been burned to the ground, the ponds and basins of the country (at best poorly watered and with no running stream between the Green and Barren rivers) had been polluted by the retreating Rebels with dead hogs, horses, cattle, and spoiled meat. Glasgow tunnel was blown to atoms as far as practicable, every good horse stolen by the Texas Rangers, bed clothes taken, and in one case under clothes of the wife of Judge Robinson in Cave City stripped from her body and burned in the presence of her family! Added to these atrocities, not half a ton of wheat, oats, corn, or straw was left on their line of flight, either appropriating the same to individual use or burning it up to prevent the Union army from getting possession of it. All the way along the route in fact- at Rowlett's Station, Horse Cave, Cave City, Cruett's Knob, Bell's Tavern, Hawkeye, and Williamsburg, with the intervening country shows the marks on incendiarism and hellish demolition.

Arriving in the vicinity of Bowling Green, you are at once struck with what would have been utter folly, recklessness, and hardihood- an attempt to take the place by an attack in front. Six fortifications are in sight from the northern side of the river, one of them and the best of which I examined carefully intended for our left flank advance is a superb work, showing more than ordinary scientific construction. It is built on College Hill where solid foundations had already been laid for a seminary; this was used as an additional protection to the fort's magazine. The outside walls with wide and deep trenches all around were made of solid rock, hewn down to a rugged steepness with palisades surrounding all, peaked and pointed, subterranean passages through with infantry and artillery could be moved at will gave egress and ingress to and from all interior points. Large cisterns filled with water, brought by slaves from the river a distance of a quarter mile were in all of them, and large pivot turntables show plainly that mammoth guns, capable of being pointed in every conceivable direction for a space of three miles would have given the law enforcers and constitution preservers a sanguinary fight had the Rebels pluck been equal to their bravado, or their spirits less speedy than their legs.

Bowling Green proper is a place of some 3,000 population but has a notoriety far exceeding its numerical strength, having been the capital of the Provisional Government of Kentucky and the best fortified by both nature and art of any place in Kentucky, not excepting Columbus. It is stated by Union citizens, many of whom are now with us as pilots, that not less than 80,000 Confederate troops were there one month ago. They have left for parts unknown, however, leaving specimens of their work the charred and ruined remains of what must once have been superbly magnificent structures- the Barren River bridge, once similar in construction to the Green River bridge, was torn down, railroad depots burned, the torch applied to the finest of warehouses, stores, and private residences. It is estimated that not less than 8,000 soldiers of the Southern army lie here in this small place, paid the debt of nature and went as victims of mercenary and unprincipled leaders to another world-many of whom had Union parents and Union sentiment- had done its work of death. One cause of the fatality among them was filthiness; another was lack of salt.

On February 27, we started for the Tennessee, arriving at the town of Franklin, Kentucky a distance of 22 miles where we bivouacked for the night and many was the poor hen shot down, Sam's boys taking them as Secesh in disguise. Seven miles from Franklin on dirt roads brought us to the Tennessee state line where piked road commences and continues all through the South. A large stone in the center of the crossroads resembling a sandstone monument tells the passersby that Gov. Charles S. Morehead of Kentucky was agreed to the boundary line and that Gov. Isham G. Harris of Tennessee was likewise satisfied. Here each band of the different regiments of McCook's division struck up "Dixie" and continued to do so until the present time. The bands in our division are those of the 1st Ohio, 5th Kentucky (Louisville Legion), 15th, 16th, and 19th U.S. regulars, 6th Indiana, 77th, 78th, and 79th Pennsylvania, 15th and 49th Ohio, 30th, 32nd, and 39th Indiana, 34th Illinois, 1st Wisconsin, and several others I have lost track of. Imagine these gentlemen all striking up the Dixie Doodle air! Was not the effect electric?

We arrived in Nashville on Sunday March 2, it having taken us until dark to march 15 miles and get over the river by slow ferriage and get to the outer part of the city, the rain through the greater part of the day coming down as if it didn't care a darn for anybody. We were marched, however, to camp a distance of four miles from Nashville and our tents and provision not having come along yet, we contented ourselves throughout a very, very drizzling rain as best we could until morning, when we were removed a space farther down the road, a camp established, and I broke for the city of Nashville. This place which by Gen. Hardee's manifests would shed every drop of blood and every cent of treasure before it would be polluted by the viper tread of the abolition shoe of a Lincoln hireling. Here can be seen in all its virgin impurity the hydra head of Secession. Anyone here a citizen can and will tell you that they are states' rights men, think the South by aid of yellow fever will clean us out, tell you to your teeth that they could raise 5,000 Rebels in their city if they could say good, and hope if the South is coerced into the Union, that she may sink into infernal regions! Such sentiments as these are given utterance any place in the city and the order of Gen. Buell that no unarmed citizen should be molested has alone prevented the delicate fist of your correspondent from coming in contact with someone's snout!

Notwithstanding what I was compelled to listen to from these not very complimentary citizens, and double prices paid for everything, change given in Tennessee scrip ranging from five cents up to a dollar (no silver), my visit was very satisfactory as it enabled me to see the 17th Ohio just embarking off steamers in which they had come from Louisville, a distance of eight days travel. I followed them to their camp four miles out on the Charlotte pike, stayed overnight in mess number one Co. A under Capt. Benjamin Butterfield, although every inch of me could have got a good meal at any place, saw everybody I known, and in fact once more thought myself at the Fashion Course Race Track! Going to town again, I saw some New Salemites of the 1st Ohio Cavalry, among them butcher Wilson, formerly proprietor of the Red Bud Rose, a first rate soldier and a jovial fellow under any circumstances. Val Culp was also along. Harman Strader and Jack Spurgeon are in the 4th Ohio Cavalry.

Seven pikes or macadamized roads lead in a southerly direction from Nashville. Mitchel's division is on the Murfreesboro pike in advance; McCook's on the Franklin and Columbia four miles out; Nelson's on the Centreville three miles out; Thomas' on the Charlotte four miles out; Wood's on the Lebanon two miles out. Each division is well supplied with cavalry and artillery. Pickets are fired on nightly by Morgan's Secesh Rangers but the recent bagging of 23 of them may convey a lesson to them and keep them at a more respectful distance than we desire. Seth Weldy is with the 18th regulars two miles from us and I am informed that he draws full ration for the men and himself.

Our company now numbers 99 rank and file- 83 present, two on detached service, two on furlough, and twelve in the convalescent barrack at Green River. Since the death of Sgt. Holtzman at the Louisville hospital, Jack Reed has been promoted to a sergeantship and bears his many honors with blushing modesty. He has not yet treated. We have more men in the 1st Ohio than in any other regiment I have seen and are likewise blessed with more field officers. Col. Smith was ordered back to his company in the regular army; Buell told him to wait for further orders; Parrott was commissioned by Gov. Tod as colonel and won't hold any position but colonel; Langdon got a commission as lieutenant colonel; Stafford a commission as major; Hooker a commission as captain, Wiley as first lieutenant, but Smith hasn't received those further orders yet, and things remain in status quo- all the regularly appointed drawing the rank from the date of commission.

The battles of Roanoke Island, Fort Henry, Fort Donelson, and the flying rumors of the downfall of Manassas have given our spirits new life and we all hope for the good of our country, for the preservation of life, the prevention of bloodshed, and the rejoicing of our relatives that the panic which has seized the Rebels may speedily terminate the war. If their arms are not lain down, we will push every armed opposer of our government into the Gulf of Mexico. It was for victory or death that we came here- we will have one or the other.

Weekly Lancaster Gazette, March 20, 1862, pg. 3

Battle of Shiloh, Tennessee
April 7, 1862

Camp in the woods near Pittsburg Landing, Tennessee
April 16, 1862

I have written no letter to anyone in Fairfield since leaving Camp Andy Johnson near Nashville awaiting the battle which sooner or later we knew must ensue.

By a rapid march McCook's, Nelson's, Crittenden's, Kirk's and Woods' divisions reached Columbia and by fording, rope-locomotion by hand, slow ferriage, and temporary bridge construction, crossed the Duck River and started towards Corinth, Mississippi where a reported stand was to be made by the Rebels. Nelson's division advanced first then McCook's and after a march of seven days with heavy knapsacks over rugged hills, on short rations, up mountain ranges and down bottomless hollows we arrived at Savannah on the Tennessee River, the loud echoing of cannon having been ringing in our ears for fifteen hours.

We (McCook's division) were embarked on large steamboats, pressed into service by our worthy general and on the 7th of April 1 o'clock at night reached what is called Pittsburg Landing where all of Gen. Grant's army stores, munitions, forage, and provisions were lying and where, too, the Rebels had driven our men within a quarter of a mile. At the time of the arrival of Gen. Buell's forces, the Rebel line of battle was within one half mile of the landing and the arrival of reinforcements to Gen. Grant was not one hour too soon. 30,000 troops, fresh from Southern camps of instruction had reinforced Beauregard on Sunday morning to make sure work of their boasted threat to drive the Lincolnites into the Tennessee River and expel the invader from the soil of the South. But the living wall of human wood that met their gaze in the morning and returned volley for volley with more than compound interest that rushed up to the cannon's mouth into the

The 1st Ohio fought as part of Brigadier General Lovell Harrison Rousseau's brigade at the Battle of Shiloh. Comer admired Rousseau's dauntless courage, remarking that the general "rode around from one end of his command to the other, apparently as unconcerned as if safely at home in Louisville." The Kentuckian grew so popular with his troops that soldiers in the Army of the Cumberland, upon hearing an unexplained commotion in camp or in the field, would attribute the cause of the racket "to Rousseau or a rabbit." [14] (Library of Congress)

jaws of death was a stamina that they had not counted on. The Rebels with an army of 120,000 men just reinforced by 20,000 more, 15,000 of their 60 days' men as bushwhackers, flushed with their victory of the day before over a force but half their number, within a half mile of our army stores, commenced an early attack, a bitter, murderous, raking fire of shot, shell, canister, and grape, a musket discharge of leaden hail which the history of other wars has never equaled.

Our division was the center, Crittenden's on the right, Nelson's on the left; that each did their part nobly I have no doubt. Justice will be done to all in official quarters- what I have to deal with is the Rousseau brigade composed of the 15th U.S., 16th U.S., a battalion of the 19th U.S., the 6th Indiana, 5th Kentucky (Louisville Legion), and 1st Ohio under the command of Gen. Lovell H. Rousseau, a noble, daring, kind-hearted, Union-loving Kentuckian who in the thickest of the fight grew not excited but rode around from one end of his command to the other, apparently as unconcerned as if safely at home in Louisville.

Deployments were made by each regiment in front. Companies A and B were sent out as skirmishers with Lt. Hooker in command, Capt. Stafford having been ordered to act as major. 500-600 yards out we came across the enemy in force; each of us fired our rifles at them and retreated to our regiment where we waited patiently for 15 minutes but no enemy appeared. We were again thrown out to scour the woods through brush and brambles, over fallen timber and muddy streams and soon saw the advancing columns of the enemy, regiment after regiment, brigade after brigade. We fell back gradually, covering ourselves with trees to the brow of a hill where one of our men, Jacob K. Hasson, received a slight bruise from a spent shell which stunned him. A double quick retreat to the 1st Ohio followed where we found our column.

The command to lie down and keep close was given when the Rebels first opened fire. This was the first regular engagement but none of Co. A were injured, although the shots flew thick and fast, one returning fire from the ground. A few minutes of suspense and then the bugle sounded the command to rise and forward; then commenced hot work and many a brave boy saw his last of earth. 'Commence firing' sounded clear and shrill, and for more than an hour and a half the sharp crack of the rifle and musket, bombs bursting, bullets and cannon balls flying, told of disrupted Union and Rebeldom, or victory and a cemented republic. Here Lt. Hooker fell, a musket ball having shattered his leg below the knee. Private William Morris was also wounded slightly. This engagement was a hotly contested one and the driving back of the Rebels was only accomplished by cool and determined daring, moral and physical courage, coupled with a consciousness of the justice of our cause. An average of 25 rounds was fired by the Rousseau brigade, and after the repulse of the chivalrous Southerners who boasted that they could whip six eastern Yankees and three western Yankees with one of theirs, it was necessary as a systematized attack had commenced on our left wing to get more ammunition from the magazine supply. Here the brigade rested in a ravine then commenced our third engagement.

Marching by the right and the left flank to the brow of a hill in the dense mass of fallen tree tops, undergrowth, leaves, and brush piles, together with passages through muddy stream and cypress swamps, the Rebels were encountered in the canyon hollow from which they poured hot shot, shell, and solid ball that made the earth shake and the heavens tremble. A vigorous and unerring fire from the Unionites with an occasional boom of the gunboat batteries made the chivalry, who to their honor as far as bravery is concerned fought like devils, start on a retreat which they did in good order. Here the 1st Ohio made a double quick charge across in the direction of the retreating enemy. To do this required a half right wheel by the regiment which left Company H of Piqua and Company A in an open field exposed to the fire of three Rebel regiments of reserve.

The repulse of the enemy from this, their strongest point, was an affair of daring and intrepid courage; the capture of the New Orleans City Battery, the finest in the South; the shooting down of the staffs and the taking of three Rebel flags; the death by an unfriendly bullet of Gen. A. Sidney Johnston, and the mortal wounding of Gen. G.W. Johnson, provisional governor of Kentucky at Bowling Green are events that will be record when the history of this rebellion is written and all of us will be proud of our part in it, but here too is where many of our men bit the dust, among them some of Fairfield's sons. Solomon E. Homan was wounded through the muscle of the left arm, Martin Schopp badly in the thigh, William Shetzley in the leg, George W. Carroll in the leg, William Morris in the head. Hasson and Morris are in the company and as well as ever. Lt. Hooker, Orderly Sergeant Homan, William Shetzley, and George Carroll have been sent to Ohio as nothing in this God-forsaken country can be found suitable for sick people to eat, drink, or sleep on. Neither are the noxious vapors continually rising from this field of blood and carnage calculated to revive the sick or add strength to the able-bodied.

Gen. John C. Breckinridge was in command of the central division of the rebel army opposed to McCook's division in the Federal army and in the hottest part of the day's engagement, Breckinridge's original brigade from Louisville and Rousseau's brigade, both Kentuckians, met. Each knew their opposition, each knew one another, and a deadly hatred exists between them. Here the 3rd Kentucky (Union) and the 3rd Kentucky (Confederate) fought each other with a desperation and zeal which one can conceive who saw it not. Two Irish brothers met, one battling for the Union and the other for disunion, and after a cordial greeting while their regiments maneuvered, returned to their commands to renew again the strife of blood. Another instance is told of an adjutant of an Illinois regiment coming across the dead body of his brother, dressed in the swarthy uniform of a Rebel lieutenant. He was first shocked, then wept, and with his own hands dug a grave and interred him. A brother's love was stronger than a brother's disgust and hatred of the Rebel cause, and an oaken slab now rests as a headstone over the dead, inscribed "My brother-gone to join the Grand Lodge above." A fact worth relating occurred to our company. Whilst out skirmishing, a rebel was noticed sitting on a camp stool with a U.S. overcoat on, in the act of shedding his old butternut colored breeches preparatory to putting on the regulation blue of the Union. Pop went an Enfield from Company A and over went Secessia's tool 'but half made up.'

As the property of the 1st Ohio preparatory to a general settlement is the New Orleans City battery and three Rebel flags of different patterns. Stafford as acting lieutenant colonel, rides a beautiful short-tailed, long-haired charger branded C.S, which means Confederate States, but which Stafford says are the initials for Capt. Stafford! Sgt. Murphy of our company has a nice captain's sword picked up on the field and several of the boys have Southern pikes, corn cutters, etc. while Edward Stober found in the camp from which one brigade was routed a full fine suit of officer's clothing. Almost everyone in the company has some little memento of this bloody battle such as fragments of shells, cannon balls, grape shot, pelican, lone star, or rattlesnake buttons, pieces of flags, bark of trees, pieces of old Confederate uniforms.

Although the 17th Ohio is left back yet on account of impassable roads, old Fairfield has its representatives here. Two companies of the 46th Ohio under Captains Henry H. Giesy and John Wiseman were in the surprise and the hottest part of the fight on Sunday, and though borne down by numbers, cut up badly, and divided from their division, the men and officers did their best and held out manfully and heroically against superior numbers. Captains Giesy and Wiseman have informed me that they intend giving you the particulars of the wounded, killed, and missing of the 46th Ohio and I leave it to them to do so as it will be more correct than what I can gather from hearsay. The 58th Ohio was also in the hottest of the fight on Monday. Two or three companies from Fairfield are in it; one company commanded by Capt. Ezra Jackson, a noble-hearted man and a true soldier who knows no flinching and is loved by his men. Squire Kinser of the Fairfield border, who started out as a lieutenant, has since been promoted to captaincy on account of meritorious deeds performed on the dark and memorable days of the 6th and 7th of April 1862. These, with Company A of our regiment, make five full companies from Fairfield. The 1st O.V.C. was also here, and Val Cupp's anxious to join Buell's company in following up the skedaddling Rebels. Added to these, Gen. W.T. Sherman (our old Cump) had command of a division continually under hot fire from beginning to end. On his staff is Lt. Dayton of the C.W.& Z. Railroad. I have also seen as visitors Aaron W. Ebright, Isaac Light, and T.W. Tallmadge.

The time our wounded were on the boats awaiting a removal northward, I went round the different bunks where the wounded were lying. One young man asked me for a drink of water; I gave it to him from my canteen when I noticed the poor fellow had his arm off close to the shoulder. He inquired where I was from and I told him Lancaster, Ohio. He remarked that Lancaster was his old home and said my name was either Little or Comer. I told him my name and he said his name was Henry Orman, an old school fellow and playmate of mine, a son of John Orman who left Lancaster some ten years ago for Iowa. Henry was just about getting a commission as second lieutenant of Co. D, 6th Iowa. Capt. Joseph Braden of the 30th Indiana was mortally wounded on Monday, a piece of shell striking him in the lower part of the stomach. He was formerly superintendent of the Fairfield County Infirmary- a good man and a brave soldier.

I know all the old camps around Washington City. I saw a great deal more than I wish to see again at Bull Run; I have read graphic accounts of the Fort Henry and Fort Donelson fights, but I am well satisfied that they were all mere skirmishes as compared with the battlefield of Shiloh near Pittsburg Landing on the Tennessee. The fifteen mile space, once known as the Shiloh Mission for the conversion of Indians, has been turned into one vast charnel house. The missing, wounded, dying, and dead of the Union force cannot be less than 12,000. At least 5,000 men and horses are lying dead on the field of Shiloh.

Weekly Lancaster Gazette, May 1, 1862, pg. 1

The regimental report of the 1st Ohio Volunteer Infantry for Shiloh shows the following casualties: 2 killed, 47 wounded, 1 missing

Official Report of Brig. Gen. Lovell H. Rousseau on the Battle of Shiloh

Headquarters Fourth Brigade, Battlefield of Shiloh, Tenn., April 12, 1862

General:

I have the honor to report to you as commander of the Second Division of the Army of the Ohio, the part taken by my brigade in the battle at this place on the 7th instant. After a very arduous march on Sunday, the 6th inst., during much of which I was forced to take the fields and woods adjacent to the highway, from the narrowness of the latter and it being filled with wagon trains and artillery and for me at that time impassable, we reached Savannah after dark. Under your orders and superintendence we at once embarked in steamboats for this place. We reached the landing here at daylight and soon after reported to you as ready for action. Under your order and accompanied by you, we marched out on the field of the day before a little before 6 o'clock A.M. Soon after, Gen. Buell came up and directed you to deploy and form line of battle, our left resting on Gen. Crittenden's right and our right extending in the direction of Gen. McClernand's division, and to send out a company of skirmishers into the woods in front. This was done at once, Major King detailing Capt. Haughey for that purpose.

Within a half hour after this you looked over the ground and decided to take a position some 200-300 yards in front on the crest of a piece of rising ground. I moved up the brigade accordingly, taking the new position indicated. In this line a battalion of the 15th U.S. Infantry Capt. Peter T. Swaine and a battalion of the 16th U.S. Infantry Capt. Townsend, both under command of Major John H. King, were on the right; a battalion of 19th U.S. Infantry, Major Stephen Carpenter, on the left of King, the 1st Ohio, Col. Benjamin F. Smith, on Carpenter's left, and the 6th Indiana Col. Thomas Crittenden on

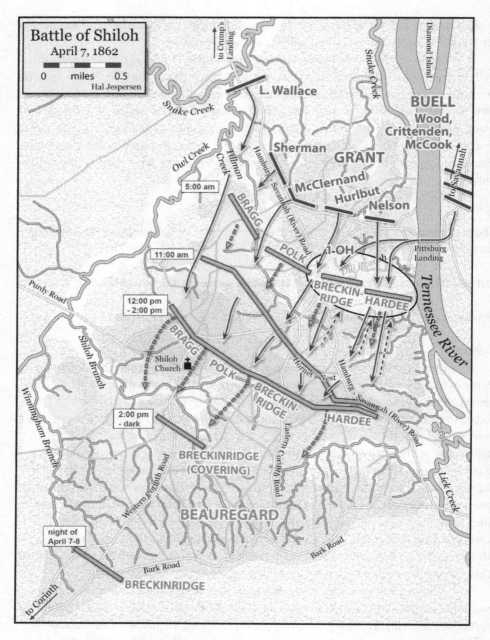

The Battle of Shiloh, April 7, 1862. Rousseau's Brigade as part of McCook's Division launched a series of ultimately successful attacks to drive the Confederates away from Pittsburg Landing. The 1st Ohio took part in three separate engagements on April 7th, helping to capture three stands of Rebel colors and a battery in the final assault. Map by Hal Jespersen. CWMaps.com

the left flank, while the Louisville Legion, Col. Buckley, was held in reserve 150 paces in rear of the line. Thirty or forty minutes after this line was formed, Capt. Haughey's skirmishers were driven in, several of his men shot, and my command fiercely assailed by the enemy. The attack lasted perhaps 20 minutes when the enemy was driven off. In this contest, Capt. Acker of the 16th U.S. Infantry was instantly killed and many others of my brigade killed and wounded. The enemy soon rallied and returned to the attack more fiercely than before, but was met by a very rapid and well directed fire from the commands of Majors King and Carpenter, and Col. Smith (1st Ohio), the 6th Indiana being out of range on the left. This attack was also, after a severe contest, repulsed and the enemy driven off, our loss being much more than before. We were ignorant of the ground in front occupied by the enemy, as it was covered with timber and thick undergrowth, but were informed that it was more open than where we were. I decided to advance my lines after this last attack and at once cautiously felt my way forward, but had not gone far when I again encountered the enemy in heavy force, and again drove him off, after a yet severer contest than any before.

About this time I received several messages announcing that the U.S. forces to our right and front, after very hard fighting which we had heard all morning, were giving way, leaving the center of the army exposed. I at once decided to move forward the whole brigade to the open ground, except the 6th Indiana, which held a most important position on our left flank, which position the enemy had menaced in strong force for several hours. I ordered Col. Buckley with the Louisville Legion to move up on the right and front and to engage the enemy, who had rallied all his available forces and was moving down upon us. At the same time, Majors King and Carpenter and Col. Smith (1st Ohio) were ordered to advance in line with Col. Buckley.

The advance was admirably made and with alacrity the brigade, steadily, briskly, and in excellent order, moved forward. We advanced about 200 yards to the front, when we came in collision with the enemy. He was stronger at this point than either of the previous encounters. I afterwards learned from wounded prisoners that the force at this time opposed to us consisted of the 3rd, 4th, 5th, and 6th Kentucky regiments, and several others from various states. The fire of musketry was the heaviest I ever heard. My line when fired on halted of itself and went to work.

The issue was important as my brigade was directly in the road of the enemy to the landing, and they were evidently pressing for that point. I was the more fully impressed with the importance of driving the enemy from this position by your words to me when you ordered a change to the front of your original line of battle, which were, in substance, that my position was in the center, and must be held at every hazard, and that you would support me with the balance of your division as it arrived on the field.

The fight lasted about 40 minutes when the enemy gave way and were at once pursued by the whole line up to the open ground in front, my brigade capturing several cannon, retaking a battery of ours captured by the enemy on the previous day, and retaking the headquarters of Gen. McClernand. We also took three flags from the enemy. At this time, the 40 rounds of cartridges in the boxes of the men were exhausted and the line was halted.

Before I resolved to advance my whole brigade to the front, I looked for the promised support and found Col. Edward N. Kirk with his brigade in my rear within short supporting distance. He told me he was there by your order to support me, and was ready for anything. He and his men were eager to move up with me. I requested that he would follow at the proper distance, which he did. After we had exhausted our ammunition, I called on Col. Kirk who was immediately in rear of my lines and informed him of that fact. He at once gallantly and eagerly offered to take my position in front and did so, a portion of my command on the right passing quietly through his lines and halting in his rear. All this was done without the least confusion or even excitement. I told him that if needed before we received ammunition, we would support him with the bayonet. The part taken in the fight by Col. Kirk and Col. William H. Gibson and their respective brigades after this and also the part taken by Col. August Willich, I leave them to narrate, with the single remark that they and their officers and men behaved most gallantly.

About this time, a battery or two or three guns-I do not know whose it was- took position about the center of my lines and opened on the enemy in front, then forming for an attack. This battery I directed Majors King and Carpenter and the 6th Indiana to support, Col. Crittenden having been just before ordered up from his former position on the left. I may here remark that the 6th Indiana in its old position had been exposed to heavy cannonading on our left and front and had lost several men in killed and wounded, and I had ordered it back into the woods. The enemy soon after advanced in strong force and menaced the battery, and its commander withdrew it; but the support just named stood firm against several times their number and gallantly beat off the enemy. In the meanwhile, a supply of ammunition for the whole command was received.

When thus repulsed, the enemy fell back and his retreat began, soon after which I saw two regiments of Federal troops advancing in double quick time across the open fields in our front and saw that one of them was the 1st Ohio, which had been moved to our left to wait for ammunition. I galloped to the regiment and ordered it to halt, as I had not ordered the movement, but was informed that it was advancing by the order of Gen. Grant, whom I then saw in rear of the line with his staff. I ordered the regiment to advance with the other which it did some 200-300 yards farther, when it was halted, and a fire was opened upon it from one of our camps then occupied by the enemy. The fire was instantly returned and the enemy soon fled after wounding eight men of the 1st Ohio. This closed the fighting for the day and a small body of cavalry was sent in pursuit of the enemy.

I need not say to you, sir that my brigade, officers and men, behaved well; for you were an eyewitness to the gallant conduct of them all and you will join me in expressing the opinion that men have seldom marched into battle under more unfavorable auspices and never bore themselves more gallantly. During the whole of the long and terrific battle neither officer nor man wavered for one moment. When all behaved so well there is little room for discriminative commendation of any. Many of them had been exposed, after great fatigue, to a heavy rain the night before on the steamboats and all of them necessarily greatly crowded so that they could not sleep and as they marched from the boats they marched through and among the 10,000 fugitives from the fight of the day before who lined the banks of the river and filled the woods adjacent to the landing, and directly on the way to our position on the field lay hundreds of dead men, mostly our own, whose mangled bodies and distorted features presented a horrible sight. Numerous dead horses and our partially-sacked camps gave evidence of the havoc and which was far worse, of the reverses and disasters of the day before.

All around them impressed them with the belief that they must fight the battle for themselves. It must not be forgotten that we fought this battle some miles within the lines of the encampment of Gen. Grant's army and in the camps occupied by his troops, and it was thereby readily apparent to the most ignorant soldier that the army had been driven in by the enemy till within a few hundred yards of the river and that the work before us all was by no means easy. Under all these unfavorable circumstances you will recollect, sir, the men were in no way appalled but formed line of battle promptly and with great coolness and precision.

To Majors John H. King and Stephen D. Carpenter of the Regular Army, who commanded the regular troops of my brigade, I am especially indebted for the valuable aid which their long experience as soldiers enabled them to render. Captains Peter T. Swaine and E.F. Townsend commanding battalions under Major King and Col. B.F. Smith, 1st Ohio Volunteers, a captain in the regular service, were likewise conspicuous for good conduct. I strongly recommend these officers to the proper authorities as soldiers by profession who have shown themselves amply fit for higher offices of usefulness. I also return my thanks to Colonels Thomas T. Crittenden and H.M. Buckley; Lieutenant Colonels E.H. Parrott, W.W. Berry, and Hiram Prather, Majors E. Bassett Langdon (1st Ohio), J.L. Treanor, and A.H. Abbott for their coolness and gallantry. Lt. Col. Parrott was on detached service at the time but joined his regiment during the action and remained with it to the close. I also acknowledge my great obligations to Lieutenants Armstrong and Rousseau, my regular aides; to E.F. Jewett, Esq of Ohio, volunteer aide, to Lt. John W. Wickliffe of the 2nd Kentucky Cavalry, acting aide, and Capt. W.M. Carpenter, brigade quartermaster, during the battle for valuable services in the field. It is due to Col. Oliver, officers and men of the 15th Michigan that I saw he joined us early in the morning with about 230 officers and men of his regiment, and behaved well during the day of the battle. Accompanying this report, you have a list of casualties incident to the battle and also the reports of the various commanders of battalions and regiments of the brigade.

I am, general, very respectfully, your obedient servant,
Lovell H. Rousseau, Brigadier General

Field of Shiloh near Pittsburg Landing, Tennessee
April 25, 1862

The loud tumult of battle is hushed, the roar of artillery is silenced, the dread missiles of death from loud-mouthed cannon have stopped their winged flight, the leaden hail of musketry has ceased. Where two weeks ago the dead and dying were scattered over the field of battle, where the wounded were lying down preparatory to passing through the dark valley of the shadow of death, where maimed and mangled humanity in every conceivable shape met the gaze wherever one turned, now all is peaceful quiet and calm repose. The rains of heaven had poured down in gushing and tempestuous torrents for four days subsequent to the deadly strife have disappeared; and now sweet, balmy spring, ever welcome, is upon us, gladdening the hearts of the jaded and weary and recuperating with its revivifying influences the physical and mental energies of those whom the hard forced marches of eight days prior to the battle, the excitement of the engagement, the ghastly sights that met the vision, the drenching showers in cypress swamp camps totally unprotected by either tents, overcoats or blankets, the short rations of five days had weakened in bodily health.

The five companies from Fairfield who participated in the fight are as lucky in point of casualties as any other I have heard of, but Capt. Stafford's company, considering the position it occupied, the fierce contest waged against the Rousseau brigade by Breckinridge's entire division, is the luckiest of all. In fact, McCook's division, at most times under a galling fire, got off from their numerous engagements with comparatively small loss. The reason why is set forth in a graphic, well written and for the most part correct communication written in the *Cincinnati Gazette* by 'Agate,' a personal enemy of McCook but one who notwithstanding this has the manliness and justice to speak as follows: 'Meanwhile McCook, with as magnificent regiments as ever came from the army of the Potomac or from any army of volunteers in the world, was doing equally well in the center. His division was handled in such a way as to save great effusion of blood while equally important results were attained. Thus the lists of kills and wounded will show that while as heavy fighting was done here as on the right or center, the casualties are fewer than could have been expected.'

Our lines of battle now cover a semicircle of about 10 miles in length with flanking and reserve brigades. Since the advent of the different divisions of Buell's army, no fears of a surprise such as drove Grant's forces over four miles and came near annihilating the splendid army of the southwest, are entertained by either officers or men. There is a deep-seated confidence in the justice and ultimate triumph of our cause and although Providence in most cases favors the heaviest battalions, according to Napoleon, a hope is entertained by us all that He will guide the war to a speedy termination and enable us to once more greet our relatives and friends around the peaceful home we all love so dearly.

We will be in at least one more bloody battle before this 'consummation most devoutly to be wished' takes place and if it be the lot of any of Company A, 1st Ohio regiment to breathe their lives out on the field of blood and slaughter, recollect them as those who knew for what they were fighting, knew for what they came here, knew the fatigue and perils and hardships to be encountered, but as those, also, who knew their duty to their God and country, and performed that duty manfully and heroically. At Corinth, the Rebels are throwing up entrenchments, building fortifications, making rifle pits, mounting guns, etc. An army of 100,000 men under Beauregard, Hardee, Breckinridge, Floyd, Pillow, and possibly Jeff Davis with the life and blood of their Potomac army, the whole recently reinforced by a column of 42,000 men from Gen. Polk's army with even 30 day men to the number of 15,000 to be rushed forward as breastworks makes truly a formidable combination against which we have to contend, but we, too, have 100,00 men here. Mitchel's division is within striking distance. General Pope's army has gone up the river; we are well supplied with all the munitions of war, well rationed, and better supplied with all the toggery that goes to make up the wardrobe of a soldier than any army in the world. We are willing in this region to make the final struggle.

Weekly Lancaster Gazette, May 8, 1862, pg. 1

Camp near Corinth, Mississippi
May 27, 1862

It is insufferably dull here just now- more so than at any other period of time other than this since the creation and the deluge-at least so it appears to one who deduces his conclusion on the presumed fact that nobody ever lived and therefore, as a natural consequence, nobody ever got lonesome here before we came. Notwithstanding the spare population in this neck of the woods, I have met several inhabitants who know the ground and situation perfectly well There for instance is:

WILLIAM HENRY MOSQUITO: a long, angular-bodied citizen with any number of relatives who, as a guide, accompanies us nights on pickets and scouts. He is well known in this locality as a person of refined taste and sensibility, eating nothing but matured army beef and drinking nothing but the best claret wine drawn from blood red sources. In business transactions he is esteemed sharp, and his smartness is proverbial and although some doubt his honesty of purpose and have striven to extinguish him, a beautiful pathetic refrain from his musical protuberance generally makes a person of imaginative turn of mind conceive a rushing river overflowing its banks and who, imagining so, exclaims damn it!

ABRAHAM WOODTICK: a scion of one of the 'first families' of Swamp Hollow, is a very peaceful little body and when once he centers his affections on a person, it is devilish hard to break his hold. Rather than prove traitor to one on whom he has become attached, he would permit his head to be detached from his body! A second cousin to Abraham paid our brigade a visit the other day and forming a liking to a soldier of our regiment, buried his head in the soldier's bosom and there it still remains. I have it from the soldier's own mouth; likewise from a huge lump on his breast wherein is contained all that was vital of cousin Wood tick! Old Abe still lives!

MR. G.NAT: is the only denizen I have seen who renders himself absolutely detestable to the soldiery. He gets in our water, bathes in our coffee, anchors on our faces, stands pickets in our eye lashes, crawls through our hair, buzzes around our ears, and goes on reconnaissances down our throats. Although Southern in tone and manners, whenever driven away by offended Federals, he immediately comes back with the assurance that he is 'for the Union as it was!'

B. CREEPER, ESQ.: is a person now held in custody by the forces of Gen. Buell, and is considered a component part of the grand army of occupation, so at least I am informed by one who was of the party that arrested Mr. Creeper as a Secesh spy, having found him under a lot of Rebel clothing left in deserted camp. He declares himself for Union, but we want nothing at all to do with him as there is no doubt but at least ninety-nine one hundredths of his friends and all his relatives are closely identified with the cotton Confederacy as they won't have anything to do with linen and wool!

Lizards, snakes, toads, scorpions abound here plentifully, but as yet I have not visited the Great Swamp to the west of us where, to use the always truthful words of Baron Munchausen, there is a three feet layer of lizards, two of scorpions, and four of toads in a boggy quagmire of 18 miles; the whole surrounded with a variegated coloring of squirming and curling snakes. For pastimes in camp, we have euchre, seven up, bluff, draw poker, horseshoe and ring pitching, wrestling, running, jumping, ration eating, tobacco chewing and drilling; once in a while, a little fight, further opponent saith not.

Musket and cannon firing has become so common along the line that the boys feel uneasy whenever they don't hear it, and the ominous silence of the last two or three days portends a heavy storm after a quiet calm, or else a more quiet calm after a heavy storm. We fill up our haversacks for a march every two days but somebody orders us in quarters and down in the region of digestion goes the rations, an easy and speedy task as one has only to mash up some crackers with an axe and then soak them in mosquitoed gravy or gnatted water.

In company with two others of our company I took a stroll over to the left wing the other day to see the company of Capt. Brown and Lt. Hewiston of the 43rd O.V.I. The men all looked well and old Peter, although laboring under a slight indisposition, was full of life, while the doctor looked as well if not better than he ever did. Allow me here to express my thanks for a glass of excellent lemonade received from them with the advice to the maker that a spike in lemonade improves it wonderfully. This makes one more lot of men (one full company and a fractional part of another) to be added to the more than respectable list from old Fairfield who will be participating in the coming great battle.

Is it not a glorious sight to see so many from our country, aided by willing hearts at home, fighting possibly with death before them for our country's preservation? Stafford's of the 1st Ohio, Butterfield's, Stinchcomb's, Ricketts', Ogden's, Rea's of the

17th Ohio; Brown's and Hewiston's of the 43rd Ohio, Giesy's and Wiseman's of the 46th Ohio, Kinser's and Jackson's of the 58th Ohio. Besides this, Fairfield has almost one full regimental staff, one full company of cavalry under Capt. Cupp, several chaplains, two aids-de-camp, two colonels, and one acting major general W.T. Sherman- all here except Col. Ewing. Aside from this is more than a full company of the 12th U.S., Van Pearce's cavalry, and Dr. Shaw of the 10th O.V.I.

Our own dear company, numbering 108 rank and file at Camp Corwin was reduced to 101 before leaving there by transfers; we have lost since by disability discharges three (Christopher F. Smith, William R. Johnson, and Eli Stoneburner), by death two (Reece Holtzman and James Colwell), and since then on the 21st of this month at our present camp Benjamin Reber[15]- making a loss of six who will nevermore return to us. Besides these, two of the transferred are dead-George W. Saylor and William Cloud. A further diminution of numbers in the 14 sick back at different hospitals- Jacob Shook, Isaac Mason, Levi Stuttzman, John H. Manler, Solomon B. Lewis, David M. Willi, Sylvester Asbell, George Fricker, George Griffith, Jacob Moore, James Smith, Edward Thornberry, Frederick Frizzell, Thomas Heist; wounded in the battle of Pittsburg and absent- Lt. Hooker, Orderly Solomon Homan, William Shetzley, George W. Carroll, Martin Schopp (reported as dying on his way by boat to Cincinnati) five. On detached service, Lt. Wiley; home on furlough Samuel Pryor Timmons. Total dead, discharged and absent 27 men, sergeant, two lieutenants. Total present 73 men, one commissioned officer leaving the second sergeant second in command. He is a devilish good fellow.

One of our company received a *Gazette* two or three months ago. Allow me to express gratitude for the same. "All quiet on the Tennessee!"

Weekly Lancaster Gazette, June 12, 1862, pg. 1

Indian Creek, Limestone Co., Alabama
(Late June 1862)

It would be very tedious to you all and likewise irksome to myself to give you all of the little minutiae and incidents consequent on the march of a grand army to this place from Corinth. Be it sufficient for me to state that we have marched over two hundred miles since leaving Corinth with heavy knapsacks on our backs. We traveled by way of Farmington, through Pillowsburg and Iuka, Mississippi, crossing Big Bear Creek into Alabama, thence to Tuscumbia on the Memphis & Charleston Railroad, where the first meal for months on the dead square that has run down my not unwilling throat was dished up by a sable son of swampdom. A tramp of five miles from Tuscumbia and ferriage over the Tennessee brought us to Florence-the county seat of Lauderdale, where more Union feeling was exhibited, or rather I should say, less animosity was shown the Union soldiers than at any other place since leaving Columbia, Tennessee. Here we pitched tents and stayed five days, the boys amusing themselves in the meanwhile by buying onions (two for five cents) and passing themselves into the provost marshal's hands. Right across the river from this place is the cave where old General Jackson and staff quartered themselves on the route from Nashville to exterminate the hostile Indians. It is a remarkable spot and the romantic scenery observable everywhere is full of reminiscences of bygone days. Gen. McCook, a second Jackson in good hard sense, military knowledge and bravery, occupied the quarters which over 50 years the hero of New Orleans evacuated. The old military road cut through marshes and woods is still to be seen, improved and rejuvenated by the extra duty men of the 1st Ohio.

On the 25th of June we left Florence for Huntsville, a distance of about 70 miles, passing through Masonville, Cherokee, and Rodgerville. To the right of the two latter places about a mile are the famous Muscle Shoals, an unnavigable part of the Tennessee River, bottomed with smooth limestone rock and dotted over with innumerable miniature cascades. The aggregated roaring of these can be heard for many miles and canoes, skiffs, and rafts can be seen drifting hither and thither by the turbulent waters, as a fisherman's harpooned gig goes down in the roaring waters. Next we came to Elk River; the bridge as usual was down; we pitched in and waded, breeches off, guns in hand, accoutrements around waists, haversacks slung to his sides, camel-backed knapsacks on shoulders. Some soldiers pulled off their shoes and the sharp gravel cut their bare feet. The captains of such were immediately put under arrest.

Next we came to Athens, Limestone County where four companies of the 21st O.V.I. were on picket. They were part of Mitchel's division and here we shook hands with Dan Richards and John Lamotte, now representing Findlay, Lt. Col. Jim Neibling was not present. Twenty miles from Athens and five from Huntsville, we arrived in our present camp on Indian Creek where Dr. Homer C. Shaw of the "Bloody Tenth be jabbers" paid us a visit. He looks hale and hearty, fat and fresh, jovial and jolly. We halted here for a few days to give red tapists a chance to show authority by way of court martial; proceedings commenced yesterday, first indictment: 'Charge- that acting orderly sergeant Harry Comer was guilty of conduct prejudicial to good order and military discipline inasmuch as the said H. Comer permitted his feet to get blistered on the march from Florence to Huntsville and was thereby unable to march two hours at a time in the hot sun at the rate of 3 miles per hour.' Hundreds of other charges of like import have to undergo examinations, some arrested for stealing geese, some for mashing their hats down, some for missing roll call, some for having sore feet, some for not having as strong constitutions as others, some for letting men get wet shoes, some for letting their men pull them off to keep shoes from getting wet.

Weekly Lancaster Gazette, July 17, 1862, pg. 2

Cowan Station, Franklin Co., Tennessee
July 9, 1862

The once glorious fourth passed off with us to the entire satisfaction of nobody. The overbearing demeanor of the recently promoted, the sultriness of the atmosphere, the compact camp guard, the rigid orders in our regiment only, the ennui of a few weeks past our absence from the actual seat of war, and the disheartening news from the Rebel capital, together with the comparisons that would naturally flow from the heart between the 4th of 1860 and that of 1862 all tended to cloud of merriment and cast a shade of gloom over our every action.

But aside from this, little oases in the desert appeared cheering us on. Major Stafford's presence (enough itself to drive away the blue devils), Dr. Shaw's and Quartermaster Lacey's sojourn amongst the boys, although requested to make their abode at headquarters, the mail from home, and the assurance that the government could and would maintain itself at whatever cost of blood and treasure were the little bright rays of the sun peeping from under the portentous clouds- the silver lining in a shade of gloom.

On the 5th we marched to Huntsville, Alabama, the prettiest place and the largest we have been in since leaving Nashville. Here is where Gen. Mitchel had his base of operations while we were at Corinth. And now a rare sight met the vision, a sight that sent the rich blood curdling hot and fast through sluggish veins; a sight that cheered our spirits and waked a huzza from weary souls- a sign of civilization in the shape of a locomotive! We had seen woods and wood ticks, forests and mosquitoes, swamps and gray backs, corduroy roads and lizards, fortifications and toads, hard crackers and snakes, rifle pits and scorpions, salt junk and mule teams, greasy niggers and dilapidated white men for so long a time that the idea of seeing ever again a regular full-grown, rip snorting, loud, screeching, big tearing locomotive engine had never crowded itself into our craniums.

From thence we went by way of Bellefonte through to Stevenson and there deviating from our original course towards Chattanooga, took the cars (yes, actually had a ride on the Nashville & Chattanooga) to this place, which, as you will see by a map, is about three fourths of an inch. All we had to do on this trip was to cut the dog fennel off the ties, sand the rail, raise and depress grade where needed, push up heavy grade, get off level grade, glide down downgrade, cut wood to fill up the tender, carry water for the boiler and crowd whole companies on platform cars. We made the distance (26 miles) in 18 hours! All we have to do now, out of companies averaging 50 privates, is to put on camp guard ten men; on railroad work such as track laying, stone rolling and bridge building, 25 men; cooks three men; water carriers and wood getters, four men; police duty, two men; on the play off and sick list, four, making 48 out of which number eight have to be taken same day for duty again to make up the guard complement of ten!

No armed Rebels (except guerillas) are nearer to us than Chattanooga at which place is reported a force of between 25-30,000 men, entrenching and command by Gen. Kirby Smith and Gen. Ledbetter. We are not only 86 miles from Nashville and after a travel of over 800 miles by the Walker line, H. Knapsack, conductor, find ourselves repairing railroad track and building bridges near Cowan Station on Boiling Fork, Franklin Co., Tennessee near where we started from four months ago! The American eagle doesn't flap his broad wings in my bosom as hard as he did once, but I have still his claws in the share of gun and bayonet.

Weekly Lancaster Gazette, July 24, 1862, pg. 3

The triumph of the 1st Ohio Infantry at Shiloh as they recapture Federal artillery on April 7, 1862. (Henry Lovie for Leslie's Illustrated Newspaper)

Chapter Four

STONES RIVER AND MURFREESBORO

Camp near Nashville, Tennessee
December 1, 1862

In order to relieve the anxiety of the '10th Corporal of Co. D, 45th O.V.I. as to the whereabouts of 'Comer,' I once more send you what little scraps of war news and war incidents I have been able to gather after my long silence- a silence wept over the secret anguish by you, no doubt; a silence with the reading public of Fairfield and the civilized world have doubtless mourned! As old Rip Van Winkle waked up on the mountainside after a slumber of 20 years, so I, after a lapse of over three months, find myself awakening from a slumbering lethargy to revive the 'sinews of thought' by another of my magnificent, rhetorical and sage epistles!

Company A, 1st Ohio Volunteer Infantry, the company and regiment who has the very doubtful honor of possessing me as a member, having been detailed as guard to brigade teams yesterday went to Nashville after quartermasters' stores. After loading up I found it convenient on my way homeward to stop over and see the 90th O.V.I. and that I was abundantly repaid for climbing the huge hill on the top of which they have their camp is a question of no doubt with either my heart or my stomach. Fairfield's boys were all OK so far as I saw; Quartermaster Jake Orman, Captains Alvah Perry and Lewis Carpenter, Lieutenants Lang, Sutphen, Sam Widener, Gus Keller and George Welsh, whole-souled, jolly and jubilant; whilst Dr. Harry W. Carpenter as if Dame Fortune was not satisfied in his case with the various promotions she has given him already (from hospital steward to assistant surgeon, assistant surgeon to principal, from principal regimental to quinine inspector of the brigade) has given him the positions of medical purveyor on the staff of General Crittenden! I do not know precisely what these mean, but some of the best trigonometryists we have in the army have figured it up in this style. Medical Purveyor: one who orders a cart load of quinine from Louisville and issues it out to brigade surgeons by the bushel. Emoluments: $198 per month.

I have not seen the 17th O.V.I. for some time but I am confident it has not been wounded in the foot since the celebrated retreat from London, the skirmish in front of Corinth, or the Bragg and Buell footrace for Louisville. The 10th Corporal can rest easy on that score for Gen. Rosecrans hearing of the vast service it was able to perform in the railroad line, set it to work clearing out the blown up tunnel near Gallatin and now, thanks to patriotic arms and Union-loving muscle, together with loyal wheelbarrows and constitutional spades and picks, railroad communication is open up to Louisville, supplies can come down to the army, officers can ride to the Galt House and friends at home can send a box of provisions and country-made socks to Co. A, 1st O.V.I. near Nashville, Tennessee almost any time they are so disposed.

Our company from having been reduced at one time down to 32 men and no commissioned officer has now 58 men present, a full complement of 'commish,' and one lieutenant in embryo or not, depends whether he gets his commission or not. One thing is certain: Orderly Solomon E. Homan deserves it. Active and attentive to all his duties, the ranking non-commissioned officer, wounded in battle whilst doing more than his duty, promised the first vacancy, he has been dallied with and cajoled, whilst others, five and number, have been promoted over him. What is the reason? Sol's father is not an influential politician; Sol's relatives have not the wherewithal to turn red tape into a Rhine wine color!

David Murphy of Co. A died in hospital at Louisville on the 24th of disease of the heart. He has a brother still in our company who, together with us all, feels his loss deeply.[16] But few deaths from disease have happened in our company; we have been luckier than most companies, but still such cases cast a shade of gloom over soldiers' hearts that the general hilarity and noisome glee of camp life cannot entirely dispel. Beauregard was superseded by Bragg; Grant by Halleck; Buell by Rosecrans; McClellan by Burnside; and Comer by Timmons! What a mighty change and still the world moves on! Who would have thought, 300,000 years ago, that on the very day Major General Burnside was placed in command of the Army of the Potomac that the second sergeant of Co. A, 1st Ohio Volunteer Infantry would get 'post of honor' in the woods of Snowy Hill? But 'time and chance, and a favoring sky, can turn a grub into a butterfly.'

We are now camped on the railroad near the Lunatic Asylum of Tennessee about 22 miles from Murfreesboro and but a few miles distant from Lavergne, where several regiments of Secesh cavalry are quartered. When the Cumberland River rises and uninterrupted communication is secured on the L&N R.R., we advance on Rebeldom once more carrying death and devastation to rail fences and creating Union feeling by robbing smoke houses and hen roosts. We will winter somewhere in the South, but next spring we will return northward to repair track, build corduroy bridges, and eat up the surplus products of Yankeedom.

Lieutenant James M. Wiley, after an absence of nine months on detached service, returned to the company a week ago, but only caught army lice on himself yesterday, all of which were left off on parole and sent south where they properly belong.

Weekly Lancaster Gazette, December 11, 1862, pg. 3

Major General William Starke Rosecrans, commander of the Army of the Cumberland during the Stones River and Chickamauga campaigns. Rosecrans reorganized the western army, christening it the Army of the Cumberland and badgered Washington authorities for better arms, better equipment, and more cavalry. "Old Rosey," while popular with the troops, developed a contentious relationship with his superiors and was undone after his army's defeat at Chickamauga and subsequent entrapment at Chattanooga. (Library of Congress)

Battle of Stones River, Tennessee
December 31, 1862-January 3, 1863

Camp four miles from Murfreesboro, Tennessee
January 8, 1863

Another great battle has been fought and won; once more has the army of the southwest triumphed. Though the Confederate ragamuffins dashed in boldly and secured the first fruits of victory, a semi-surprise, still do the Union banners float in, around, and about Murfreesboro, the last grandstand point of the C.S.A. against the army of the Cumberland.

From the very hour the different corps of our army left the suburbs of Nashville in their advance into Rebeldom, they were badgered and bushwhacked, dashed at by cavalry, guerillaed by riflemen and shelled by mountain howitzers, Secesh firing and then retreating to another hilltop. Meanwhile the armies of the Union moved steadily on in line of battle to within about four miles of Murfreesboro and took up their assigned positions in line, intending to move on the entrenched position of the Rebels as soon as the bulk of our army had arrived. On the 30th of December, all but one division had got to the ground. Cavalry fighting had been going on at the outposts all day and men of opportunities for knowing predicted a grand fight on the morrow. The night of the 30th was cool and breezy, but the rising sun of the morning of the 31st was bright and brilliant as if no armed hosts were lying face to face like crouching panthers ready for a spring. Our division (the Second) under command of Gen. Johnson was quietly eating their breakfast when a courier arrived at each regiment with the order to 'fall in-double quick-the enemy is advancing!' Orders were obeyed promptly, but the foe had already driven in our pickets, captured a full complement of battery horses and two guns from one of our brigades without opposition-the horses just being watered at the creek.

We were in McCook's corps and on the extreme right wing. Here the enemy, in order to turn our right flank had massed at least one half of his strength and we, having but a single line of battle with a regimental reserve for each brigade, had but a poor chance, yet that poor chance was improved. Major Joab A. Stafford was in command of the regiment and handled it until our being driven in, as well as any man possibly could. We were in a kneeling position behind a cedar rail fence and our brigade (the Fourth) maintained its position against four visible lines of battle, twelve pieces of artillery, and dozens of sharpshooters ensconced in treetops for 35 minutes. We gave way and retreating at a slightly augmented double quick to the woods, rallied in ones and twos behind heavy cedar thickets and picked off the advancing columns of the enemy until their steady and impetuous rush was checked by our reinforcements, who turned the tide of battle, enabled the disorganized to reform and do as brave and heroic fighting as any army of volunteers in the world has ever yet done or will ever do.

For four days after the battle, or rather series of battles, it was purely strategy. Yankee tricks, night skirmishing, masked batteries, changes of base and advances, with fortifications and counter fortifications- until the crowning bayonet charges of Saturday night the 3rd into the rifle pits of the enemy which drive them from their position and decided the six days' battle of Stone River near Murfreesboro. As official reports will give you all the information of general movements, I will only give you the casualties of our own company and companies D and I of the 90th, who were in Van Cleve's Division of Crittenden's corps, and fought with a steadiness worthy of veteran troops. They were on the left wing and although no large bodies of butternuts in mass assailed their lines, they at least had abundant room for hard work and severe fighting.

Of our missing, we can hear nothing at all. Young and Rockey were the last to leave the battlefield and as the Rebels followed us up on our retreat of Wednesday morning the 31st, we fear they are either killed or prisoners. We buried only those in front of our own division line; none of our missing was among the number. I will give you incidents and scenes of the battle in my next-some of which would move a heart of stone, and bring tears to eyes of all 'unused to the melting mood.'

Weekly Lancaster Gazette, January 22, 1863, pg. 1

The regimental casualty list for the 1st Ohio at the Battle of Stones River shows the following: 8 killed, 47 wounded, 81 missing, Total: 136

Stationed as divisional reserve behind the Union right, the 1st Ohio fought a short but desperate battle against troops from Cleburne's and McCown's divisions. The regiment splintered into squads on the retreat with many of the men captured by troopers from Wharton's Cavalry Brigade near the Wilkinson Turnpike. (Battles and Leaders)

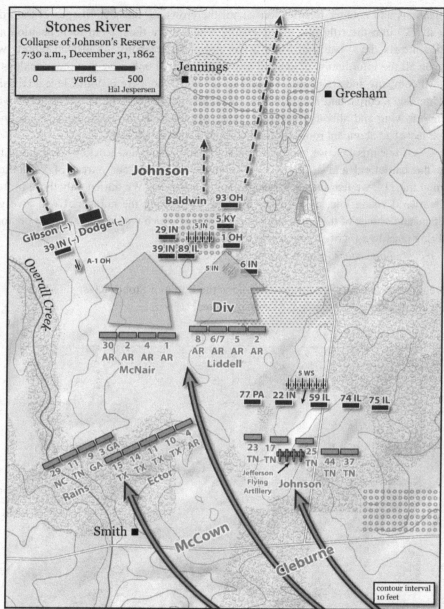

The 1st Ohio fought as part of Col. Philemon P. Baldwin's brigade at Stones River. "We were in a kneeling position behind a cedar rail fence and our brigade (the Fourth) maintained its position against four visible lines of battle, twelve pieces of artillery, and dozens of sharpshooters ensconced in treetops for 35 minutes," remembered Private Comer. Map courtesy of David T. Dixon and Hal Jespersen.

Official Report of Major Joab A. Stafford on the Battle of Stones River

HEADQUARTERS FIRST REGIMENT OHIO VOLUNTEERS, In Camp, January 5, 1863.

CAPTAIN: I have the honor to report the part taken by my regiment in the recent battles and skirmishes about Murfreesboro.

On the morning of December 27, 1862, when about a mile below Nolensville, the enemy appeared in our front. I was ordered by you to form a line of battle on the right of the pike, my left resting on the right of the 6th Indiana, and deploy two companies as skirmishers, and to advance. I did so, deploying Company B, First Lt. Henry Dornbush commanding, and Company D, Lt. George L. Hayward commanding. We had severe skirmishing all day, but drove the enemy before us, and encamped near Triune.

On the morning of December 30 we were ordered to join our division, which had preceded us the day before, within about 4 miles of Murfreesboro. We arrived about 4 o'clock, and, after making a reconnaissance on our right, we fell back and bivouacked for the night in a piece of woods in the rear of our division.

On the morning of the 31st, about 6.30 o'clock, I heard what I thought to be heavy skirmishing on our right. I immediately ordered my command under arms, and marched to and halted on the edge of the woods just to the right of where we bivouacked the night previous. A few moments after, by your orders, I moved forward at a double-quick across a large open field, and formed my line behind a rail fence, on a line with the 6th Indiana [they occupying a piece of woods to my left], with two pieces of Simonson's battery between us, the 79th Illinois and 30th Indiana occupying a piece of woods to my left], with two pieces of Simonson's battery between us, the 79th Illinois and 30th Indiana occupying the right, the 79th in reserve.

I ordered Lt. Hayward, Company D, to deploy the first platoon of his company as skirmishers. This had hardly been done when the enemy appeared in our front in three distinct lines of battle, followed by columns, closed in mass, several batteries of artillery, and a large amount of cavalry, the left of their lines extending not less than one fourth of a mile to the right of the 30th Indiana. As soon as they arrived within about 150 yards of my line, I opened fire, which checked their advance for about fifteen minutes. Their line then in front of me seemed to separate, and I saw them marching by the flank to the right and left of us. Immediately after this maneuver, the two regiments on my right gave way, and left my flank entirely unprotected. The enemy's left then changed their front to the right and marched diagonally toward my right. At this moment the 6th Indiana was forced from their position, the enemy immediately taking possession of the fence they occupied. They then again appeared in my front and opened an enfilading fire on my regiment.

Finding it was impossible to hold my position without being annihilated, I ordered my regiment to fall back, intending to take a position in the rear of the Louisville Legion, which was at that time supporting me. My regiment started back in good order, but coming in contact with the Louisville Legion [Colonel Berry having just ordered a change of front forward on first company, to protect our right], we became entangled with them, as we did also with the 93rd Ohio, which you had ordered to our support. I then fell back in some confusion to the woods occupied by me some half an hour previous.

Here I tried to form my line, but again became entangled with a part of the First Brigade. My regiment became scattered, and it was impossible to get them into line until we had fallen back through the woods into a cotton-field and into another piece of woods. Here, by your help and the united efforts of my officers, I succeeded in rallying part of my regiment, and took position on the left of Colonel Berry, who had also succeeded in rallying part of his regiment. Here the enemy was checked and driven back a short distance, but soon rallied and came down in a solid mass, and we were obliged again to retire.

In a short time after, I rallied a portion of my regiment, and meeting Captains Nicholas Trapp (Company G) and Patrick O'Connell (Company F), who had succeeded in doing the same [in all, amounting to about 100 men], I halted and formed a line. Here I was joined by a portion of the 93rd Ohio, under the command of Lt. Harman. I took command of the whole.

At this moment I received an order from Gen. Johnson to proceed immediately to a certain point, but the guide missed the place, so I took a position on the left of a regiment [I do not know what regiment] which was hotly engaged with the enemy. Here I remained until I was ordered to fall in the rear of General Rousseau's division.

Soon after, Col. Anderson, of the 93rd Ohio, came up and took command, and was ordered to proceed in the direction of the river; that we were needed there. Word soon came that our division was again forming on the left of the railroad running toward Nashville. I immediately proceeded to that point, where I found about 100 more men of my regiment, under command of their respective officers.

By your order, I again moved forward with the balance of our brigade to the support of another brigade, which was hotly contesting the ground we now occupied. After a short and severe fight the enemy were driven off, and with considerable fighting and skirmishing it has been held ever since.

The loss in my regiment is heavy, so far as heard from-8 non-commissioned officers and privates killed; 1 officer and 46 non-commissioned officers and privates wounded, and 81 missing; a partial list of which you have already received.

My officers and men behaved most gallantly, and I do not think there are any soldiers in the world that could have done better under the circumstances. I would most respectfully recommend for your favorable consideration Captains Kuhlman, Company B, acting field officer; Nicholas Trapp, Company G; Patrick O'Connell, Company F; Capt. George A. Pomeroy, Company E; Capt. Benjamin F. Prentiss, Company H; Emanuel T. Hooker, Company A, and Alexander T. Snodgrass, Company I; First Lieutenants Henry Dornbush, Company B, commanding, and George L. Hayward,

Company D, commanding; Adjutant Samuel W. Davis, and Second Lieutenants Anton Kuhlman, Company B, commanding Company C; Robert B. Chappell, commanding Company K; Dennis Denny, Company G, and First Lt Alexander Varian, not yet assigned to any company. They are all justly entitled to the thanks of their superiors for their gallant conduct in the past few days. All have been engaged in the service since the breaking out of the rebellion; have been in several engagements, and proved themselves worthy the confidence reposed in them. A more gallant and braver set of officers never entered a field. I would also mention our surgeons, Doctors Albert Wilson and Jacob C. Barr. They performed their duties faithfully and unflinchingly.

I had forgotten to mention that sometime during the day a portion of my regiment, under Lt. Dornbush and Adjt. Davis, gallantly repulsed a charge of the enemy's cavalry, and drove them off altogether.

Very respectfully, your obedient servant,
Joab A. STAFFORD,
Major 1st Regiment Ohio Volunteers, Commanding.

Camp near Murfreesboro, Tennessee
February 1, 1863

Since writing you last, death has claimed two more of our company. Sylvester Asbell, one of the largest and stoutest men, died on the night of the 14th of typhoid fever in the city of Nashville. To say that he was one of our best and bravest soldiers would be but re-echoing the sentiments of everyone in our company. As was said by one of the company who witnessed the death scene, 'he died in the Grace of God, singing, and shouting' and now rests in that bright and gorgeous realm were war's alarms and hideous paraphernalia are unknown. Nimrod A. Webb, another of our company and one, who like Asbell was a man with wife and children, died of the severe wound he received in his shoulder at the battle of Stone River, and his soul has gone to the God who gave it. He, too, was a soldier of no common merit. Prudent and phlegmatic in action, taking his standpoint from a mature deliberation, less impetuous than most of his comrades, he was always prompt, steadfast and reliable and combined the qualities of a gentleman to that of a punctual and remarkably clean soldier.[17] Rest in peace Sylvester, Nimrod farewell! No one who suffers and dies in the cause of his country, for honor, for love, for the future, and for God suffers or dies in vain.

James W. Bennett, Freeman M. Wolf, and Jack Reed all left Nashville on steamboats and at last accounts were doing as well as could possibly be expected. They will all recover shortly from their wounds. All three were among the best if not the best soldiers in our company. The flesh wound received by Bob Shannon is healing fast and he will return to duty in a few days.

There are no indications of a fight soon in our immediate front. We (Johnson's Division, now under command of Col. William H. Gibson of the 49th O.V.I., formerly

Ohio's financial disburser) are encamped four miles from Murfreesboro on the Shelbyville turnpike. Our foraging parties, consisting of one brigade, go out six or seven miles further and nary an armed Rebel is seen; but just let a small force of say a regiment or couple companies of cavalry go out and they will either be compelled to get up and skedaddle or else fight superior numbers and get ticked, their forage train taken, and themselves sent to Chattanooga!

A Sanitary Commission came down from Fairfield to see the surviving and attend to the wounded and dead of our county after the battle of the cedars on Stone River. Jared T. Hooker called on us in the night. We were sent on picket next morning before day. That's the only peep Company A, 1st Ohio Volunteer Infantry, Capt. E.T. Hooker commanding ever had at one of Fairfield's 'sanitaries.' Our company since its organization has more in killed and wounded than all other companies from Fairfield put together (aside from Grant's Department) and if friends from home could make it convenient to call on us every third visit, they would be treated with all the civility and decorum to be found in camp etiquette.

Col. Edwin A. Parrott of the 1st is now in command of the brigade, Col. Harvey M. Buckley of the Louisville Legion having gone into the Kentucky State service as an acting brigadier. Lt. Col. Langdon is still on detached service as inspector general on McCook's staff, leaving Major Stafford still, as for a long time back, the actual colonel although two grades less in rank. Whilst on this subject, I will mention that justice, tardy and long delayed, has at length been done to Solomon E. Homan, for a space of 16 months our orderly sergeant. Entitled to the second and possibly the first vacancy occurring in our regiment, he was put off and put off with empty promises until several sergeants received their commissions. One for him at length came, dating from October 25, 1862; he received it about three weeks since and day before yesterday was appointed adjutant. From the dirty, greasy, dilapidated inhabitant of a dog tent, he is now promoted to the first class berth of adjutancy-mattresses and quilts for bedding with luxurious grub and palatial delicacies to drive away the thoughts of hard crackers and fossil flitch, fat, fair, and four times forty. Officers like him who have worked themselves up by their own exertion, without the aid of army snobs or citizen soldiery, who have seen the injustice and ingratitude often shown enlisted men by what are termed superiors are not liable to forget old associations or tyrannize over the rank and file. Adjutant Homan, after Capt. Hooker was wounded at Shiloh, took command of the company. At the late battle, Hooker being lame, the command fell again upon him but I fail to find either in our then Col. B.F. Smith's report of Shiloh[18] or Maj. Stafford's recent report of the battle of the cedars, one word of praise as to his prowess, although severely wounded in one battle and manfully showing his heroism in the other. Then he was only an enlisted man, and couldn't do anything meritorious; now he is a 'commish'- all he does will be carefully noted.

We are patiently waiting the approach of the individual known by the appellation of division paymaster. Payrolls for two months have been made out but our worthy Union owes us five, we expect to get four. Retrenchment and reform, pinching economy should be the watchword and rule of action of the Treasury department. Would it not be politic, therefore, to defer payment of troops until another big battle? Many of those who are now fighting battles of the country are men of no families-having enlisted in companies away from home, their messmates do not even know the place they came from (especially is this so among the Regulars). Now, kill off a lot of these men, have company officers postpone sending off final statements until doomsday of the others that fall in deadly strife and Uncle Samuel can come out all OK- making bounty, back pay clear and clean on each one. This I am confident would be a great saving. Maybe the government is trying my suggestion now; it not, let it send the greenbacks on- we can get rid of them, but not the gray backs. Greenbacks pass away as dew in the summer's sun; gray backs hold their own and don't go off worth a mill dam!

If anything rears its head, turns up, shows itself, or promises a fight, I will let you know in my next-that is, if I don't get up and skedaddle as I did the other day or Hooker don't have me on extra duty as usual. Great men will differ; Hooker and I can't agree I don't see why; I have always considered myself a good looking, intelligent, very well drilled, a fine soldier in all respects, of good shape, docile, obedient, while extreme modesty has several times gotten me into bad predicaments. But here, without doubling, I come to a right face, arms port, break ranks, march! 'One man for guard tonight!' Who will it be? I see my worthy successor approaching, so that guard will be Harry Comer. [19]

Weekly Lancaster Gazette February 19, 1863, pg. 3

Camp Drake, Murfreesboro, Tennessee
March 23, 1863

Since writing you last, nothing of note has transpired worthy of your readers' attention. Everything in the news line is as stark, stiff, and dead as the broken axle of a dead cart or a defunct specimen of blessed martyrdom. Why then do I write? Simply to let you know that I am still alive, able for duty so far as ration eating is concerned, and although paid off but recently, am already prepared for another mass of greens.

I have just said that things are dull here-by this I mean monotony in camp. Right inside the entrenchments, in town, a different view is presented. Hundreds of swearing drivers, bulky mules, creaking wagons, loud mouthed officials, laughing niggers, emancipated east Tennesseans, Union refugees, Secesh spies, and citizen soldiers from the northern regions anxious to escape the conscription give one an idea of the busy season in Cincinnati around Rat Row and the levee. At the depot is a perfect pandemonium of confusion and bustle if one can credit his own eye sight. The rattling of trains arriving every couple of hours, their departure, the loading up of sick, unloading of reinforcements, ammunition, and grub, the peanut, apple, orange, lemon, pie, and cake stands, controlled by dark browed Ethiopians of Anglo-Norman descent, and venturesome merchant princes in Union blue-together with horse traders, Peter Funks, Jeremy Diddlers, confidence men, draw poker, three card Monte, over and under, Honest

John, old sledge, and chuck-a-luck (all anxious to make themselves heard and felt) reminds one very forcibly of the Pickaway Races or the closing days of the Fairfield County Fair.

Our picket line was drawn in the 20th some two miles-Secesh in the bush found it out, told Van Dorn, Van Dorn thought we had evacuated this point and came to us with a rush but went back with a mammoth flea in his ear at a quadruple quick multiplied by two, leaving nearly an entire brigade of chivalrous Arkansans as hostages in the hands of Sheridan's division. Rosey hadn't evacuated worth a 'continental cuss.'

Myron Gregory of Lancaster came down here on a flying visit the other day with Capt. Goulding, stayed fifteen minutes, flapped his coattails and flew back again, not having time to spare to visit the camp of the 1st Ohio or even that of our Light Battalion which, according to General Rosecrans' order, is made up of three men in each company of the regiments of a brigade 'most noted for conspicuous bravery and daring courage, for soldierly conduct, endurance, skills, and proficiency in the use of firearms, to be selected by ballot of their comrades and recommended by their company commanders. These are to be 'looked upon as the elite of the army and counted the models of their profession.' Such is the mere outline of the qualities of the men composing the Rolls of Honor in the various brigades. William Heberly, George M. Myers, and Charles E. Grandlienard received the honor from Co. A of the 1st Ohio-an honor well deserved and which all freely accord them.

Our detachments are made from the 1st and 93rd Ohio, 6th Indiana, and the old Louisville Legion, and a better looking set of men never entered the field. Brave men selected, of course a brave field officer must be in command and where a braver than Joe Stafford of Bull Run, Day Ridge near Perryville, Pittsburgh Landing, and Stone River notoriety? He was selected by the big guns and gives universal satisfaction as he has always done, whether lieutenant of Home Guards, captain, major, or commander of our regiment.

A little merriment was created in Murfreesboro on Sunday last by the marriage of Christian Frazer of the 42nd Illinois to Matilda Ann Williams, a young miss of this place of only 40 summers. She is possessed of a house, lot, and a few niggers, which will in part compensate for her lack of youth and beauty. 'There never was a goose so gray, but some day, soon or late, an honest gander came that way, and took her for his mate.' Direct papers and letters to acting commissary and quartermaster sergeant and sergeant major Harry Comer.

Weekly Lancaster Gazette, April 2, 1863, pg. 3

Captain Henry Dornbush of Company E was cited in official reports for staving off a cavalry charge at Stones River on December 31, 1862 while a lieutenant in Co. B. Dornbush was wounded in the leg at Chickamauga on September 19, 1863 and again at the Buzzard's Roost in May 1864. (Larry M. Strayer Collection)

The following letter, unlike the rest of the correspondence, was written to Private Jack Reed of Co. A, 1st Ohio Volunteer Infantry, who was home in Lancaster recovering from the effects of a wound sustained at the Battle of Stones River.

Camp Drake, Murfreesboro, Tennessee
April 6, 1863

Old Jack:

I must apologize to you for not answering your letter sooner. In fact, I had not over two hours per day to myself to do so, and those two hours were taken up by me in the enjoyment of the various pastimes which abound so plentifully in camp at the convivial gatherings subsequent to an army pay day!

We have at length recovered some from the saddening scenes of the battle of the cedars on Stone River; no longer is the fierce booming of the cannon heard, or the direful rattle of musketry, no longer do the fiery war horses gallop past in mad fury, and no longer do panic stricken soldiers with distended eyeballs skedaddle over the corn and cotton fields from insatiate Seceshdom; no longer is heard the hoarse voices of the great captains and giant colonels urging on us on to glory and renown, the victory or death. Scenes of blood no longer meet out gaze; the bloody wounds, the gaping gashes and distorted visages, the livid and ghastly countenances of the unburied dead, the gory pools of clotted gore have all passed away and now a serene tranquility and calm repose marks the spot where so many yielded up their souls to God and reddened with crimson tide the sanguine field of Murfreesboro.

Moved back from our advanced position on the Shelbyville Turnpike, and we are now snugly ensconced in the immediate front of the breastworks and fortifications commanding this noted and historic town. The entire Army of the Cumberland, an army that has never yet experienced defeat, is stretched along for miles in three parallel lines so that when reveille's shrill bugle notes arouses us from slumber in the morning, three living walls of bristling bayonets present a formidable barrier to any force the grease-encased chivalry can hurl at us. In all my knowledge as a soldier or citizen, in all the various incredible spectacles which have met my sight the last few years, there is none equal to our line of battle these fine, balmy, and refreshing morns of spring. Imagine, Jack, a line of battle on an open plain of which you can see neither beginning nor end, then conceive that line three deep of armed impetuous hosts willing and anxious for the next grand battle in which they see the solution of our country's troubles. The whole capped off by thousands and thousands of snow white tents and cedar groves and you can form some estimate of the awful grandeur, sublime beauty, and grimaced paraphernalia of the moving panorama each day enacted in this locality. Our company and regimental parade grounds are kept as clean as any business house in Lancaster, the debris has all been removed and were it not that we know that a few miles further on death awaits many a poor soul, we would think ourselves fairy spirits of a brighter realm on a brief visit to the 'vale of tears.'

Notes of preparation are, however, beginning to be heard; the signs of the time augur important events. Convalescents are coming to their regiments; citizen soldiers are taking the places of soldier clerks and confiscated contrabands the places of teamsters; all detailed men are ordered to their companies while straggler and deserters come pouring back to us on every train. In the meantime, hard bread, bacon, beans, sugar, coffee, rice, and salt form a perfect tower near the railroad depot and if it is not quite as high as the Tower of Babel, it must be nearly so while I am confident that confusion of tongues is no better. Here in one conglomerated mass can be seen in the course of an hour English, Irish, Scotch, Welsh, Prussian, Russian, Polish, Swedes, Persians, Spaniards, Frenchmen, Germans, and Hollanders together with the indomitable progressive Yankees, all vying with each other as to who can make the most noise, make and render confusion still yet more confounded. This babelism is confined, however, to the dark browed sons of Ethiopian nativity and eastern Tennessee refugees whom the government has employed at the military depot of supplies.

Light battalions have been formed in various brigades of this department to be composed of three of the very best men in each company of a regiment of each brigade. Charley Grandlienard, Billy Heberly, and George Myers received the honor, by ballot of their comrades from our company- a compliment to them and us. I was placed in the battalion as quartermaster sergeant by Major Stafford, but Hooker saw Langdon, Langdon saw Parrott, Parrott saw Johnson and the result of their combined seeing was that I was ordered back to the regiment and tomorrow I report for duty to Colonel Applegate of General Hooker's staff![20]

How is your wound getting Jack? When will you be back to the regiment? It will be our pride and delight to clasp you once more by the hand and welcome you back to your country's service, knowing as we do, that the blows you strike are struck from patriotic feelings-not that dastardly love of country seen only in the almighty dollar.

And now in conclusion, dear Jack, let me hope that the beams of peace may shed their heaven-lent rays on us all before the pass of another month and that you and I and the many other impulsive hearts that have stood with their breasts to the foe to guard our country from irretrievable ruin may meet around the social boards at home to rejoice over the dispelling of war's alarms and a Union made more stout and refined by having passed through the ordeal of fire and blood.

Weekly Lancaster Gazette, May 14, 1863, pg. 1

Chapter Five

ONWARD TO CHATTANOOGA

Camp Drake, Murfreesboro, Tennessee
June 5, 1863

I have been waiting for something to turn up for so long a time that I have got tired of waiting and shall run the risk of your displeasure by again addressing you.

Since writing you last, our regiment has been reinforced by four recruits from Fairfield- George W. Brock, sutler, Charley Kutz, assistant, Jack Reed and Sam McCleery, clerks, Joshua Lamotte, coachman-making things look for this locality for the first time decidedly Lancasterian. Brock as a businessman and a gentleman has already gained the good will of the regiment, and a better regiment for sutlering; don't drill four hours per day and do fatigue duty between times. Charley Kutz, with his conviviality of disposition amuses all hands with his quaint descriptions of California life and the Golden Elephant, whilst Jack Reed, fresh from hard tack and bean soup,[21] dispenses commodities in a soldierly manner. These three, as you may imagine, constitute a whole team, the wagon and the harness, but when you place old Joshua Lamotte on the box and give him the reins, the firm is complete, and so all aboard for Shelbyville. Fat Sam McCleery of Greenfield is also here as clerk and makes and excellent appearance, being three feet two inches across the breast.

Don't imagine for a moment, dear *Gazette* that I am writing this for the purpose of elevating to my lips the delicious nectar of the Bacchanals at Brock's expense, 'tis merely to give you an idea of the vast estimation in which I hold their Root & Butterfield principles.

We have had nothing very interesting or exciting in this latitude lately; in fact, it has been quieter than at any time during my recollection. The last few days, however, have been different and the seeming lethargy is coming to a close. Our picket lines have been strengthened; our outposts and the different avenues to this place are now more carefully guarded whilst our reconnoitering parties invariably meet the enemy a few miles out on either route. What this means, I know not-it may be that, tired of waiting for us to advance, Secessia is coming to give us battle, drive us back into our fortifications, storm our breastworks, scale the walls and tumble in on the shrieking Yankees, cut off our cracker line, and hold a regular carnival over Yankee bean soup. But while they are at it, we will most probably see them and enter a solemn protest. On the other hand, it may be merely a ruse to deceive us into that belief whilst they are leaving Tullahoma. Even whilst writing this, the loud booming of cannon in the direction of Franklin to our right and on our front towards Shelbyville tells of more than a mere skirmish, and we are all under orders to march at a moment's notice.

Our pickets are now on duty with knapsacks, shelter tents, clothing, and seven days' rations, ready to join their respective divisions at the picket line. At the time of Bragg and Buell's foot race through here last fall, all we had to carry was on our backs and in our hands, our money and rations being in our pocket books- now we go with a full lot of clothing, knapsack, gun and accoutrements, shelter tents, three days rations in our haversacks, four in our knapsacks, and two in our hats, and a million bushels of everything in the rear which will be protected by a sufficient force to repel any marauding force of Morganites who may see fit to try an assault in the absence of the main army.

Convalescents and exchanged prisoners are still coming in, about 300 having arrived today for our division alone; tomorrow, our brigade will be reinforced by about 200 more who are now in Louisville. This will make 500 for Johnson's division of the right wing, who are all war-stained heroes from the fields of Shiloh, Chaplin Hills, and Stone River, who will amount to more effectively than two full regiments of new recruits or conscripts. Forced back the morning of the 31st of December last, many of them return with revenge burning in their bosoms, and that you will hear good accounts of all, there can be no doubt. The 17th Ohio is still at Triune; the 90th Ohio on Cripple Creek, each having the same orders relative to marching as ourselves. Hooker is still captain of Company A. When Capt. Stafford was promoted to the majorship, Hooker as first lieutenant got the captaincy, which made him tenth in rank. He is now fifth in rank, with the prospect of fourth; the old captains resign one after another in order to give him a chance.

We are very well supplied with grub here, but I occasionally have an extra meal forced on me by Lt. Gust. Keller of the fortifications; Lieutenants George Cormany and Holmes of the 6th Ohio; Col. Jim Neibling, Lt. Dan Richards, and sutlers Tom Richards and Jim Clifford of the 21st Ohio, which I accept with alacrity, devour with avidity, thank them in felicitous language, wishing them many happy 'returns of the joyous occasions!' The most magnificent present I have yet seen in the army was made to Col. Neibling by the non-commissioned officers and privates of the 21st Ohio. It was a two edged sword, with sash, spurs of solid silver, belt, field glass, etc. The scabbard is solid silver and it is inscribed the Colonel's famous battle command at Stone River to his regiment of over 900 men-'Go in twenty-onesters, and give 'em hell by the acre!'

I have just received a *Gazette* which tells me that Bob has been superseded by Abe. The outgoing and incoming have my best wishes for future success. As Abe is a poet, I will give him some of my own verses, knowing that he can appreciate them. Here goes:

As I have nothing more to write,
I will hand this pen back to the feller,
I got it of, and say good night!
The Lancaster Gazette, June 18, 1863, pg. 1

Steamer Glide, off Fort Donelson, Tennessee
August 3, 1863

Many little items of note have doubtless transpired since my visit home from the Department of the Cumberland- enough most likely to fill a small book which will be written by me on my arrival at the regiment. I shall have time to do so without doubt, as I have already intimated at Cincinnati and Louisville that the 1st of August has already past, and that furloughs written out at Paris are not current anymore with Rosey's provost marshals. Brothers Clarke, Fritter, Bickford, and Drake will please not accuse themselves of dereliction of duty on my account, for however garrulous I may be on some subjects, to them, I was as mute as a mouse on one certain topic.

My object in writing this letter is purely complimentary to the citizens of Fairfield, who throughout my entire sojourn amongst them, treated me as a human being and a gentleman, treated me with courtesy, distinguished deference, and sour beer, and whether hereafter my lot is the guard house, my fate a bullet, or (my preference) a skedaddle from danger, I shall look back on the time spent in old Fairfield (but 10 days) as the beautiful oasis in the desert of soldiering. In fact, all classes and conditions, heroes, sheroes, wild Irish, dumb Dutch, blacklegs and cutthroats, Republicans, Democrats, Wolly Heads, Butternuts, Abolitionists, Copperheads, Nigger Lovers, and Straight-out Locofoces, vied with each other as to who could do me the most honor and show most respect for the bright and shining luminary who wrote so many 'really love letters' to the otherwise torpid columns of the *Gazette* from the grand armies of Buell and Rosecrans.

Whatever Lancaster may be in common times, it surely was in a stir whilst I was there: three days of militia business, one of riot, one of circus, one or two of Democratic outpouring and in pouring, two or three little fights, and any amount of copper distilled patriotism. I missed the picnic on account of not being able to get a horse and buggy, Uncle Crist telling me that 'army fellers didn't know how to drive!' Don't, eh? And now, *Gazette*, I'm about wounded up. We start in a few minutes for Nashville, run all night and will get there some time tomorrow night, where I shall deliver over to Jimmy Lyons, Manny Richards, and George Washington Wilkinson the several packages I have for them, and then start for Tullahoma.

It may be proper before I close to say something of the steamer *Glide*, the boat on which I am making this trip. It is an elegant light-draught passenger packet, although small, and as neat and comfortable as any that runs the Cumberland River. She makes through trips to Nashville from Cincinnati and is under the management of Capt. W.B.

Anderson and J.H. Porter; two as accommodating men as one has ever traveled with. By the way, a little anecdote may not be out of place here: William Latta of Lancaster is in the Ordnance Department at Louisville and on bidding me 'good bye' at the Galt House, cautioned me to be sure and continue my letters to the *Gazette* as they were read with immense interest. I told him I should do so. J.H. Porter, clerk, was standing by and inquired of me how long I had been employed in the *Gazette* office. I told him four years. Says he, the *Gazette* does all our printing. I then saw his dilemma, how many horns it has I don't know, but he and the captain, thinking me the travelling correspondent of the *Cincinnati Gazette* for four years and therefore a good one, are excruciatingly kind to me in all that pertains to the cabin saloon! They are expecting a 'puff' in the *Cincinnati Gazette*; what will they think when they see it only in the 8 x 10 of the Hocking Hills!

Once more, I tender my compliments and regards to the people of Fairfield, and if they ever take a trip of the river of green backed frogs, huge pollywogs, deadened dogs, old rotten logs, sand bars, snags, etc., let them take in on the *Glide*!

The Lancaster Gazette, August 20, 1863, pg. 1

Tullahoma Guardhouse, near Hooker's Company, Tennessee
August 15, 1863

Once more I address you. From this secluded retreat, I seat myself on a dilapidated mess pan with a cracker box for my escritoire and a pen likely used at the time of the signing of the Declaration of Independence as my only writing facilities. Hoping you will pardon the shaky hand that directs the said antiquated pen, I will close my introductory by assuring you that the shakiness is not caused by any 'spirituous or malt liquors, wine, or cider,' those articles were all drank the first night of my arrival by a set of loafers who kept me awake until nearly four o'clock in the morning.

One distressing incident occurred in Company A in my absence. James Wesley Bennett, who was wounded at Stones River and returned to the regiment some six weeks after, was killed by the explosion of a lot of Secesh shells near the depot in this place which, by some sort of carelessness, ignited. He was a good soldier and a brave man, prompt and efficient in duty, and worth at least a half dozen soldiers such as me.[22] Lieutenant Charles Young is not yet mustered in as a 'commish,' an order against mustering in having been issued until companies are recruited to the minimum. He will be mustered as soon as Company A receives ten drafted men, and eight have already arrived. One of them last night wanted to know when the battle was to be, and how soon the bushwhackers would be in town, supposing we had regularly stated periods for our fighting.

John Strentz of Co. D, 90th Ohio is here in the hospital, suffering with a severe attack of chronic diarrhea. John has friends and relatives in Lancaster and I would advise them to get him away from this division as the medical surgeons of this locality, anxious to gain knowledge by practical experience, have on several occasions amputated soldier's legs to cure them of a toothache!   William Doty of Lancaster, express agent on the

Chattanooga & Nashville railroad between here and McMinnville, gave Co. A an entertainment yesterday by way of getting his foot bruised between the bumpers of two cars. It was a narrow escape from crushed bones and the people of Lancaster can congratulate themselves on being able to see him again in future.

Major Joab A. Stafford has been strongly recommended by the officers of this division for the colonelcy of the veteran battalion, but he labors under the disadvantage of having no influential political friends to rush him through. Rich daddies can place their sons on the top ladder over merit. The veteran corps is to be raised up from the old troops now in the field who are to enlist for three years from date, and are to have in addition to the first service perquisites a bounty of $400 and a premium of $2, to be paid in installments. This would bring a private's pay the last two years up the savings of the 'commish,' especially where the commish plays poker and drinks mean whiskey at two dollars per bottle.

Corporals Poulton and Shannon have returned to duty from Nashville after a severe illness looking better than ever. The last seen of them today was at dinner making sad havoc of two or three pecks of roasting ears, which Bob found out on picket last night at a Rebel commissary's. George Macklin of Palentown, is here in the sutler department under G.W. Brock. He is attentive to business, accommodating to all, and very regular in his habits, having been present at every meal since his arrival.

I cannot close this desultory and rambling epistle without giving you a description of the 'round about' here from where I am sitting. To the left, as far as I eye can see (about four feet) can be seen a wall of plaster, well tinged with tobacco spit, to the right a twin brother of the other, artistically frescoed with gigantic cobwebs; to the rear, a huge mass of rags and blankets facetiously termed bedding; to the front, a glistening line of bayonets, reminding me forcibly that war is going on- a fact which very few of Fairfield's unterrified fully appreciate. Around above and below, wood ticks, flies, and mosquitoes swarm and flutter but we old soldiers who go home on 'French's' don't mind such little things as them. Lice are very scarce.

Political topics do not engross much attention, yet I am surprised at the number of Vallandighammers here. There are about two in our own corps and I heard of another in Thomas' corps- he, however, belongs to Indiana and will have no vote in Ohio when we elect Brough. The boys look at matters practically, not theoretically. They think if the war can be whipped to a termination in six months after the conscripts reinforce us, we will get home somewhat sooner than if we waited until the succession of a Democratic president next 4th of March a year.

Hoping this letter may compensate for any tardiness heretofore, I close with the wish that the Rebels will not bother the railroad on which our rations are carried.

The Lancaster Gazette, August 27, 1863, pg. 1

Private Comer languishing in the Tullahoma Guard House (Abby Kitcher)

Weed patch No. 3287, northwest corner Alabama cornfield
September 1, 1863

I notice in the late numbers of your paper that colonels so-and-so, captain this and that, and lieutenant somebody else arrive occasionally in your city. I fail to see you notice, however, the arrival at any time of Sergeant Knapsack, Corporal Mess Pan, or Private Dog Tent. I assure you, however, that they are a very important part of the department and are almost as effective as 'commish.' I myself, home ten days, saw nary a notice of my distinguished arrival or hasty departure. May the Lord forgive you.

Since writing you last from Tullahoma Guardhouse, I have been 'redeemed, regenerated, disenthralled,' and by the blessed power of universal emancipation, for when the order to march came, your worthy correspondent was loaded with dog tent, gun and accoutrements, haversack, and three days' rations and together with my beautiful compatriots, a deserter, a victimizer, a drunkard, and a horse thief, took my place in the ranks. Over hills and hollows, bogs and fens, swamps and streams, rivers and mountains, a distance of 94 miles, we at length arrived here, only 42 miles from where we started. We are now gathered around the base of an infernal big hill called the Sand Mountain, and if we ever get up to the top, then we will be in Georgia. Our generals are now deliberating as to whether we will go up by taking the wagons and gun carriages apart and carrying the pieces by hand, a la Napoleon, or whether we will ascend by the block and tackle process.

Nothing of note transpired on the march; nothing 'turned up' but dust; nobody was hurt other than with bruised shins and blistered feet. I could not fail to observe the utter demoralization and 'ruthless vandalism' of the soldiery. Our short-sighted commanders, thinking to camp in the shade, placed us in potato patches and peach orchards, near young corn fields, and although grub was short, Johnson's men had long capacities and pound after pound of the delicious products of the sacred soil of Alabama and Tennessee took their melancholy flight down the great gateway of pork, beans, and lager beer. From observations taken in the states mentioned, I have come to the conclusion that the state of Tennessee is more hospitable than that of Alabama, from the fact than in the former state citizens furnished us with cedar rails for firewood and in the latter we are forced to take oak!

September 3, 1863

At length we are up but when we shall get down is merely a question of time. Worn out mules and jaded horses strew the wall all along the loosely-bouldered ascent, but a breathing spell is here given us to enable the rear guard to catch up. Today, a soldier of this division was dishonorably discharged from the service for conduct 'prejudicial to good order and military discipline.' He forfeits 'all pay that is now or which may hereafter become due him'- a hard blow as his last year of service had already commenced. The baggage of all officers was today reduced to regulation limits, and we have now but three wagons to a regiment-one for headquarters and officer's baggage, one for forage, and one for cooking utensils, grub, and extras of ten companies. Officers are allowed to have hauled one sheet of note paper and two small wafers, but as they have 348 days yet to stay on the three years contract, they bear it uncomplainingly.

September 5, 1863

We have marched to the foot of our rugged and jaded mountains, and are now encamped in Pearson's Gap of the Sand Mountain, which like Larkin's Gap of the Cumberland range, must have been made as a nigh cut to the infernal regions. But we will appreciate the beauty of not getting any lower down and console ourselves with the thought that in 11months one week and four days, our time will be up.

September 7, 1863

Still at the same place with a prospect of staying a day or two longer. A lieutenant of the 93rd Ohio had his sardine boxes taken off his shoulders today in the presence of his regiment and sentence read, endorsed by Rosecrans, that he should be forever debarred from holding office of trust or profit under the government and was summarily dismissed from the service. He however had about two years to stay yet. His offense was refusing duty and speaking disrespectfully to his superior officer.

September 8, 1863

Preparations for a forward movement-one division to go over Lookout Mountain, the other to go around it; which division (Davis' or Johnson's) will have the honor over going over the sandstone peaks of a higher promontory than where Fremont caught the bumblebee I'll tell you in my next. By that time, it will be warm work or else no work at all, for Lookout is but nine miles from Chattanooga and divisions or corps are always thrown ahead to protect a place more effectually. The provost guard house is now doing a thriving business and recruiting is going on steadily- no less than 14 new men having enrolled themselves yesterday. They are all entitled to an escort and bear the honors with unblushing modesty.

Stanley's division of cavalry, embracing the very best mounted men of the service, passed us on this route and is somewhere in the advance, endeavoring to capture Rebel forage trains and break up Rebel railroad connections. He has a competent force with which to do it, and if his own force is insufficient, McCook's corps will do the balance.

We have heard of the Union sentiment that pervaded the mountainous regions of the South so long; we have heard so much talk about the sturdy mountaineers who would throng to our standard in long and loud huzzahs at once more beholding the old flag; in short we heard so much and saw so little of loyal men in the Southern states that we had come to the conclusion that is all a miserable hoax boxed up inside of a mammoth lie, but in the sterile waste of rockiness we just passed through, a pure, pure, and loyal sentiment obtains and is not a mere outburst of fear or obsequiousness. As instances, heads of two families have reported to division headquarters for passes to go to Illinois, at the same time inviting all Union soldiers to take whatever they could find on their places, as otherwise it would fall into Rebel hands. One widow woman with a family of eight sons has seven of them in the Union army, four having joined us on the mountain. But one half mile from here a Rebel conscripting officer lies in his grave, a bullet having pierced his breast, fired by a mountaineer who now marches to the step and keeps time to the music of the Union.

All is well in Rosey's department so far as I am able to ascertain and the stirring events which will soon take place will reach you by telegraph or railroad if such things are in these parts long before the graphic delineation comes from my humble pen. But how is it among you at home, are you all right on the goose? Are a majority of you opposed to this war of self-preservation, or are you like Artemus Ward the showman, 'willin' to sacrifice the hull kit of yer blud relashuns for the blessed Union?' We have heard with humiliation and disgust the sacrilegious outrage perpetrated at Amanda by prominent Vallandighammers and if hell with its torments was gaping wide before them, many in this army would insist on a few more wagonloads of brimstone as the full rations for such men. It is an old dogma, however, of politicians that parties invariably become corrupt where there is no opposition to them, and if religion and Christianity were not assailed by their opposite, might degenerate into their own vile type of treason.

Men of Fairfield! You who have fathers, brothers and sons in the army; you who have near relatives and dear friends, you surely will not turn your backs on those who came out with your sanction and advice, who have stood for over two years with their faces to the foe, between you and war's desolation, as a living wall that the screeching shell, the leaden hail of death, the murderous steel, might bend but could not break? Bring down the rebellious majority to 800, speak out as freemen, pay no attention to the intriguing wiles of politicians, and when election day comes around and we can execute the privileges of freemen (and who has a better right?) you will find out that our opinion of the Union by those harmless missives which 'come down as still as snowflakes on the sod, yet execute a freeman's will as lightening doth the will of God.' Then Fairfield will be redeemed; then too, Fairfield's sons will not be ashamed to own their birthplace or residence and will send up from the mountains of northern Alabama or southern Tennessee or from the plains of Georgian cotton fields, one long deep and jubilant huzza for emancipated mind and a perpetuated Union. Blessed be the day when the shackles shall fall from the party serfs of otherwise noble old Fairfield and all unite on the broad and substantial platform or 'equal rights and Union-now and forever.'

This letter dear *Gazette*, as you will observe, was commenced on the 1st of September when we had 11 months and two weeks to serve as Uncle Samuel's nephews in 'crushing out the monster rebellion, maintaining the constitution, driving back Rebel hordes, etc.' It is now the 8th and we have only to stay properly 343 days more but that confounded leap year comes next year with the odd day in February. How many hours will it be? Let me see: 344 days, 24 hours per day, 8,256 hours or 49 weeks and 23 hours!

When I will get this letter off I don't know-nobody knows. Mail facilities are not the best just now owing to the bad roads or no roads at all rather, no post office, no mail carrier, no spare mules to send back, nor no nothing. Rest assured that as soon as practicable, this communication shall speed on its winding and devious way to the haunts of white man and the regions of civilization.

The Lancaster Gazette, September 24, 1863, pg. 1

Battle of Chickamauga, Georgia
September 19-20, 1863

Chattanooga, Tennessee
September 27, 1863

Another great battle-the bloodiest of the war and one which, had it been brought to a successful termination on our part, would have placed the hydra-headed monster of Secession on the block of the guillotine, has been desperately fought and although victory has not perched on the banner of beauty and glory, all have an abiding confidence that final success will be ours, and that the grease-encased hordes of Rebeldom who for the last two weeks have bushwhacked us in the mountains of Tennessee and Alabama, thronged the gaps and swarmed in the woods and corn fields of Georgia will at length feel the freemen's might and tremble at the power which subdues them.

Previous to the main body of Rosecrans' army leaving the sandy ridges of Raccoon Mountain, Chattanooga had been occupied by Crittenden's Corps, Bragg's force having retreated to Crawford's Creek ten miles over the state line. Rosecrans having at length found out where the valorous braggadocio had gone, resolved to attack him in his stronghold among the mountain fastnesses of his native state and on the 18th struck the enemy's left. Deploying troops in a line so as to cover Bragg's front, Rosecrans gave him battle and at many points along the line drive him two or three miles. The battle raged from early morn until 5 p.m. when a lull ensued, the shrieking shell, the whizzing grape and canister, the fierce rattling of musketry and the deep-toned reverberation of cannon's roar through mountain gorges, ravines, and canyons gave promise for that day at least the work of death had ceased-that the angel of mercy was visiting the scene of carnage. But a wild, shrill whoop from 45,000 throats, the entire length of the line, the myriad hosts of gray backed legions that came on a double quick charge, pouring their leaden hail into our ranks told, and unmistakably too, that the short space of time between that and nightfall was the turning point of the day's strife, and that a hecatomb of lives would soon saturate the ground with its gory sacrifices.

Eight massed lines of gray and steel! Miles of flashing flame! 45,000 human beings bent on human destruction! Before them a living, breathing, palpitating wall of

Major Joab Arwin Stafford, Harry Comer's original company captain and his favorite officer. Stafford led Company A until June 1862 when he was promoted to major. Stafford led the 1st Ohio through Stones River and again took command after Lt. Col. Langdon was wounded at Missionary Ridge. Major Stafford served the final year of the war as colonel of the 178th Ohio Volunteer Infantry, leading it through engagements in Tennessee and North Carolina, and was brevetted as brigadier general of volunteers in 1865. Stafford's competent leadership, earnest care and respect for his men was enough, Comer wrote, "to drive away the blue devils." (Generals in Blue)

anxious hearts-anxious for the coming of the foe, anxious for the Union's fame and glory, yet likewise anxious for those far-off sisters, brothers, fathers, mothers and friends who in the distant north knew not of the sanguinary strife where so many sank exhausted, where so many laid to die. Flesh and blood weakened by a series of marches over the roughest roads and bypaths it has ever been my lot to travel. Our left flank crumbled into nothingness; our center gave way; the right was compromised and the hard-earned laurels of the day passed from our grasp in less than three fourths of an hour! Reserves were brought up, the enemy checked, a new line formed, and the dark pall of night fell over the scene of secession's joy and a nation's tears.

Sabbath day broke forth bright and beautiful, not a cloud of darkness cast a shade of gloom over the luminary whose resplendent rays shone on northern and southern alike. The turbulent engines of destruction for a space were stilled, the chirps of either belligerent force paying mute homage to the day of rest, but a little picket firing on the flanks, a few scattering shots in the center, then a volley of musketry on the right-another and another- and now the loud-mouthed cannon belching forth its fire and smoke rends the very air, and the struggle has commenced! No wonder the contest is bloody in the extreme; no wonder it was prolonged without cessation the entire day, no wonder it exceeded in vindictiveness and desperation any battle heretofore fought in this department. Chivalry was fighting for the key that unlocks the door to all the able-bodied Negroes of the South; fighting to whip Rosey's little army of 50,000 effectives before reinforcements could arrive, fighting their last fight, if defeated, in this department. Freedom fought for nationality, for honor, glory, fame, for equal rights and the God-given inheritance of man. After a series of most hotly contested engagements, successful assaults, gallant repulses, with dead and wounded scattered over miles of mountain land, the grand Army of the Cumberland gradually and mile by mile withdrew here, experiencing for the first time a partial defeat, and losing a victory whose good results would have been incalculable to the Union.

We are now around and over Chattanooga, have entrenched ourselves and the rebellious hordes, elated with a partial success over the army of the southwest (an army that has never before experienced one solitary, single reverse) are going through the farce of a siege at very long range. But thanks to spades, picks, axes, and bouldered embankments together with the Rebel fortifications we compelled them to abandon, aided by a firm determination to do or die, we have completely checked the advancing wave of the combined forces of Bragg, Johnston, Buckner, Breckinridge, and Longstreet's corps from eastern Virginia, with probably part of A.P. Hill's.

The Rebel loss must have been tremendous-ours was proportionately heavy. Official reports will give you the generalities and plan of battle. I shall only give you casualties in our own regiment, remarking that no division did better than the Second Division of McCook's corps under Johnson, nor no brigade did better than the Third under Col. Philemon P. Baldwin of the 6th Indiana.[23] It maintained its old renown and held ground against superior numbers many times during the last ten eventful days. Lt.

Col. E. Bassett Langdon of Cincinnati was in command of the 1st O.V.I. and showed himself a man of nerve and valor; Major J.A. Stafford, as usual, proved himself a genius on the battlefield, whilst all the line officers without exception gained additional laurels to those already acquired at Shiloh, Chaplin Hills, and Stone River- Lt. John W. Jackson of Co. I being killed, and Capt. Henry Dornbush (Co. E), Lt. George J. Grove (Co. F), and Lt. Gustav Hallenberg (Co. K) wounded. All honor to the noble dead, who on the altar of their country, have given themselves as sacrifices. Though words of consolation may be vain to those who have lost a son or brother or a near and dear friend, those at home can rest assured that the memory of our messmates who fell in the deadly strife is embalmed in the heart of hearts, and a grateful country will not forget their untimely fate when war's alarms are over and peace, conquered by the strong right arms of valiant souls shall once more bless us with heavenly joys.

Casualties in the 1st O.V.I. total 14 killed and 129 wounded. In Company A, four killed, 13 wounded, and one missing. I shall endeavor to find out particulars and give them to you in due course of time, if living. Rebels can be seen all around us, but today we are burying dead under flags of truce.

The Lancaster Gazette, October 15, 1863, pg. 1
Harry Comer's father Isaac Comer died back home in Lancaster the very day Comer wrote this letter describing the battle of Chickamauga.

In a scene typical of the dense woods of the Chickamauga battlefield, Confederate infantry attack Union positions. The 1st Ohio held position near Winfrey Field throughout the afternoon of September 19th before their right flank was turned and the regiment forced to retreat. As at Stones River, the 1st Ohio fought against troops under the command of Gen. Patrick Cleburne, one of the finest Confederate commanders in the Western theater. (Battles and Leaders)

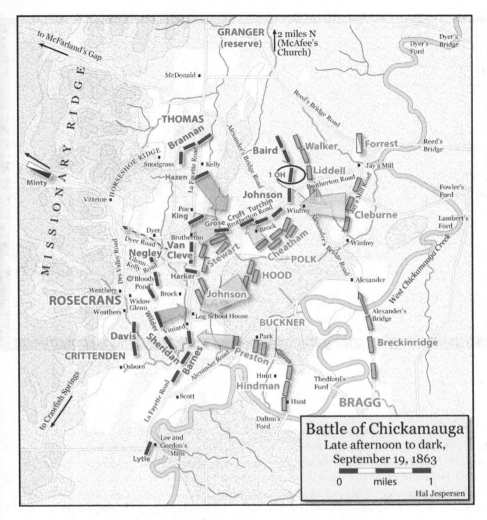

The Battle of Chickamauga, September 19, 1863, late afternoon through evening. The 1st Ohio, as part of Col. Philemon P. Baldwin's brigade (circled), took part in a series of engagements for the control of the Winfrey Field on the Union left. The Confederate assaults here were among the most vicious of the battle; late in the day, the 1st Ohio was driven out of this position and fell back to the La Fayette Road. Map by Hal Jespersen. CWMaps.com

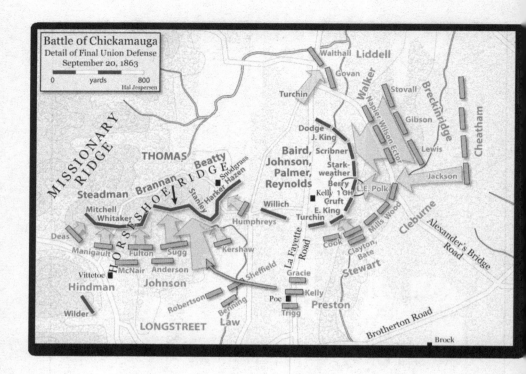

The Battle of Chickamauga, September 20, 1863, morning through late afternoon. The 1st Ohio, driven back from their position near Winfrey Field late on September 19th was sent into the Union line defending Kelly Field. An attack by Adams and Stovall's brigades against the left of the salient prompted the 1st Ohio to be pulled out of line and sent towards the rear to drive out the victorious Confederates. "The brilliant charge cleared the woods in our rear and taught the Rebels a lesson of caution which saved us from molestation," reported Lt. Col. E. Bassett Langdon. The regiment lost 14 men killed and 129 wounded in the two days' fighting at Chickamauga.
Map by Hal Jespersen. CWMaps.com

Official report of Lt. Col. E. Bassett Langdon of the Battle of Chickamauga

Headquarters, 1st Regiment, Ohio Volunteer Infantry
In the field, September 27, 1863

Captain: By direction of the colonel commanding the brigade, the following report of the operations and loss of the 1st Regiment Ohio Volunteer Infantry is respectfully submitted from the 18th instant to the present time.

On the morning of Friday the 18th instant, the regiment moved to the front under my command and took position in line of battle, relieving the 105th Ohio. Three companies were at once advanced as skirmishers to within sight of the enemy and shortly after, it being ascertained that no connection existed on our left, five more companies were moved out and a regular picket line established, connecting the 93rd Ohio Volunteer Infantry on our right with a shifting line of infantry pickets to our left.

This position was occupied until the morning of Saturday the 19th instant, our picket line sustaining most of the time during the day an irregular and distant fire from the pickets of the enemy without returning it. The regiment withdrew from this position early Saturday morning under marching orders and moved about 10-12 miles up the valley to the north and east and were halted in an open field near a tannery under the fire of the enemy's cannon. During the few minutes that we lay there, one man belonging to Co. K was mortally wounded and died the next morning.

Being ordered forward, we moved rapidly to the front in double-quick time and a quarter of a mile farther on I deployed in line of battle on the left of Gen. August Willich's brigade, my regiment forming the right of the first line of the Third Brigade. A platoon of skirmishers from each of my flank companies (B and G) was deployed in front of the regiment and moved forward to find and feel the enemy. Two hundred yards sufficed to bring them under the enemy's fire, and I moved the regiment up rapidly, keeping even with the first line of Gen. Willich, halting when his line halted and advancing as he advanced.

The enemy fell back steadily and rapidly before our advance and were hotly followed up and pressed by the skirmish line. The enemy abandoned a battery on the right of my line which was taken in charge by Gen. Willich's brigade in whose immediate front it was situated. After pressing the enemy back about a mile and a half in this manner, I halted my regiment agreeably to orders in an open field of weeds, with my right near the woods and my left advanced diagonally across the field fronting to the east with from 100-300 yards of open descending ground in my front, terminating in a ravine, beyond which was an open forest into which my skirmishers had followed the enemy. Col. Baldwin shortly afterward ordered me to change front to rear on the first company and retire behind the fence on my right, information having been received from Major Stafford, in command of the skirmish line (now strengthened by the remaining platoons of the two flank companies) that the enemy was moving to our left.

But a short time elapsed after this disposition was made till the enemy precipitated a heavy force upon the regiments on our left, closely followed by an attack in our front and upon the brigade on our right. I opened fire by file as soon as our own skirmishers were clear of our front, and soon drove the enemy back from the open field and well into the woods, when, finding myself free from fire, and that the enemy was directing his whole attention to the regiments on my right and left, I sounded the signal to cease firing and again moved into the open field where my fire would be more effective against the enemy.

This position was held till the enemy was repulsed all along the line and had fallen back beyond our fire, when, by order of Col. Baldwin, I again took position behind the fence and strengthened it by a hastily constructed barricade of rails. Major Stafford was again sent forward with skirmishers into the woods beyond the open field. Companies A, C, and G were detailed on this duty under their respective commanders, Capt. Emanuel T. Hooker, First Lt. Thomas W. Boyer, and Capt. Nicholas Trapp. Co. G which had skirmished from the beginning of the action, was soon after relieved by Co. E under command of Capt. Henry Dornbush. Information was sent me that the enemy was now moving to our right which was promptly communicated to Col. Baldwin. About sunset, my skirmishers were pressed back with serious loss to within a few yards of the regiment where they were exposed to so hot a fire from the enemy that I recalled them to tempt the enemy into the open field. In this skirmish, Capt. Dornbush was seriously wounded in the thigh and the command of his company devolved on First Lt. George P. Leonard.

Finding the enemy not disposed to enter the open field and the firing having increased on my right, I sent Co. A again into the field as skirmishers to prevent the enemy from getting too close to my front unobserved, the nature of the ground being such as to raise an apprehension of that character. This company was in the act of deploying when it found itself exposed to a very hot fire on its right flank, and immediately took position to meet it and opened fire warmly in return. At this instant Gen. Willich's regiment, on my immediate right, opened fire in line and warned by all these indications where the real attack would come, I hastily recalled the skirmishers, intending to meet it by a volley at short range. Unfortunately, the recall of the skirmishers, who fell back firing, and the heavy roll of musketry on our right with the whistling of the enemy's bullets set the guns of my right company going and an irregular file fire ran along my front from right to left, mainly directed to the enemy in my front. Meantime, I strove in vain to make myself heard to stop the firing and call the regiment to attention. In 30 seconds, the regiment on my right was broken and running to the rear in great confusion and while I was striking my men (who were lying down) with the flat of my sword to get their attention, the Rebel line was seen within 40 yards of my right flank moving rapidly perpendicularly to it. I was barely able to get my men to their feet in time to see the Rebel colors flaunted almost in their faces and their guns being mostly unloaded, I directed them to retire. The regiment fell back about 150 yards and rallying handsomely on the colors, delivered a withering fire on the enemy, which checked his advance and drew in return a storm of grape, canister, and musketry. The contest raged till long after darkness and the dense smoke of battle had shut out everything in view but the flash of the enemy's guns and only terminated when the enemy ceased to return our fire.

During the fight, the sound appeared to indicate that the regiments on our left were being pressed back and I sent First Lt. Robert B. Chappell (Co. K) to ascertain the state of facts there and assure those troops of our ability and intention to hold our own. I sent the same officer to the right to communicate with Gen. Willich and his report relieved me of apprehension in both directions. On the termination of the fight, I learned from Gen. Willich than an order has been issued for the Second Division to fall back, which I communicated to Capt. Strader of Col. Baldwin's staff and in half an hour, the regiment retired at the head of the brigade to the place where the knapsacks had been deposited on entering the fight.

Bivouacking there until morning, I was ordered to take position in line of battle on the left of the brigade in the second line and construct a breastwork for defense. A substantial work was soon built and hardly completed when the enemy opened a fierce attack in our front. So suddenly did it burst upon us that Capt. Hooker, in command of Co. A as skirmishers, was unable to get back to the regiment and fought till the enemy was repulsed behind the breastworks of the first line. Twenty men were detailed from my command to man the guns of the 5th Indiana Battery who fought with it during the day. In the intervals between the attacks of the enemy in our front on Sunday, I had usually one or more companies of skirmishers covering the front under the command of Major Stafford who had charge of the skirmish line of the brigade.

About the time enemy made his second attack in our front, and while my command was moving to relieve the 93rd Ohio on the first line, it was discovered that the enemy had broken through Gen. Baird's line on our left and filled the woods to our left and rear with his troops. The open field between us and these woods was covered with fugitives in Federal uniform fleeing the victorious enemy. Under the command of Col. William W. Berry (5th Kentucky), I at once about faced and changed front to oppose them, and almost immediately afterward moved forward, recrossing the breastworks of the second line into position on the right of the Louisville Legion and opened fire upon the enemy, checking his advance and driving him instantly to the cover of the woods. With one impulse and apparently without command, the entire line rushed for the woods.

I turned to see if the movement had been ordered and received Col. Berry's order to halt and return my regiment to its proper position at the breastwork. My voice could not be heard in the confusion and seizing the colors, I had the halt and "to the colors" sounded by my bugler and succeeded in getting about two-thirds of my regiment into line and back to position. The remainder went on ignorant that a halt has been ordered and took part with the Legion and 15th Ohio in the brilliant charge which cleared the woods in our rear and taught the Rebels a lesson of caution which saved us from molestation, when later in the day they again broke Gen. Baird's line and entered the same woods.

Among the losses attending this charge I have to report Second Lt. Gustav Hallenberg, seriously wounded in two places; First Sgt. Burgdorf, Co. B, mortally wounded, and a number of my bravest men killed and wounded. When ordered to retire in line of battle, my regiment moved off at the double-quick and in good order, and although subjected to an enfilading fire from the enemy's batteries, accomplished the movement with a loss, though unknown, was certainly smaller than would have been thought possible. A half hour sufficed to place us safely on the hills in the rear and no further loss was sustained by the regiment until the following Tuesday, when it was placed in an exposed position on the bank of the creek south of Chattanooga and endured the fire of Rebel shells and solid shot from batteries on our flanks and front for the space of about one hours time. By this fire or by the fire of the two guns of the 2nd Minnesota Battery, situated in the rear of our right flank, two sergeants and four privates were wounded. The wound of Sgt. William D. Miller of Co. C was terrible and mortal. He died in a few hours after. On that evening, the regiment was retired to a batter position and a strong breastwork constructed on that night and the following day.

On Thursday, a reconnaissance of the front was made twice by Major Stafford, Capt. Hooker with Co. A, forming part of his force on the last and Capt. William J. Patterson with Co. H on the first occasion. The first was without loss but the last cost the death of Private John McCarthy, Co. A, and the wounding of John Shannon, also private of the same company. The regiment continued in front till Friday evening when it was ordered to the rear, and after eight days and nights of duty under arms and under fire, was permitted to enjoy the rest it much needed.

In all these varied duties of picket reconnaissance, skirmish, battle, and siege which the experience of these eight days covers, my command behaved admirably; always vigilant, patient, active, and brave. Officers and men deserved victory and obtained it, for they were successful throughout-uniformly so. Some cowards there were among us, it is true, but only enough to make brighter the example of the brave men of the command.

To the officers and men of the regiment I generally tender my sincere thanks for their good conduct. To the valuable services of Major Stafford and Capt. Trapp, the senior captain present, I am much indebted; both are experienced soldiers of tried courage and ability. The regiment sustained a heavy loss. First Lt. Jackson was killed by a grape shot on Saturday night while gallantly waving his sword and encouraging his men. Capt. Dornbush and First Lt. Grove were wounded seriously on Saturday afternoon. The latter rejoined his command on Sunday morning but was unable to continue with it. Second Lt. Hallenberg, whose conduct is always admirable, was separated from his command in the pursuit on Sunday and wounded in the woods to our rear. He rejoined the company afterward but was compelled to leave it on the retreat. Fourteen in all are known to have been killed, 80 are wounded, and one officer (First Lt. and acting adjutant Charles N.

Winner) and 40 men are missing. Among the missing are doubtless many killed and wounded and probably some prisoners. Among the killed are Sgt. Andrew Losh, William B. Riddle, and Corp. Robert M. Taylor of Co. G; Sgt. William D. Miller, Co. C, and Private James H. Springer, Co. I. Privates Caleb Copeland and John McCarthy, both of Co. A, deserve special mention for their gallantry. We need not stint their praise. No after act can sully the brightness of the record they have left.

Please find the accompanying list containing the names of the killed and wounded. Thirty-eight prisoners were taken by my skirmishers on Saturday and turned over to the provost marshal of the brigade.

I have the honor to be, captain, very respectfully,
Bassett Langdon, Lt. Col. 1st Ohio Vol. Infantry, commanding regt.

Lieutenant Colonel Elisha Bassett Langdon of Cincinnati had been elected to the Ohio House of Representatives at age 25 and served three terms before being elected to the Ohio Senate just before the outbreak of hostilities in 1861. Langdon took part in the battle of Shiloh with the regiment then served as inspector general for Gen. Alexander McD. McCook's division and later corps. Returning to the regiment after Stones River, he led it in its desperate battles to secure Chattanooga in late 1863. Large of build and commanding of presence, Langdon was severely wounded in the face and neck leading his men in their successful charge at Missionary Ridge. Private Comer described Langdon as a man of "Herculean proportions" and admired his "nerve and valor." Langdon died in 1867 at the age of 40 from the complications of the wound he sustained at Missionary Ridge. (Larry M. Strayer Collection)

Battles of Orchard Knob and Missionary Ridge, Tennessee
November 23-25, 1863

Missionary Ridge, around Chattanooga, Tennessee
November 27, 1863

Since last I wrote you very important movements have taken place in this department. This opening of the railroad and river communication to Chattanooga from Bridgeport, the junction effected with Hooker, the arrival of Sherman, the passage of the pontoon fleet past the Rebel batteries studded the grim and rugged sides of Lookout Mountain, the flank movement which compelled the evacuation of the northern slope, the many skirmishes on the Wauhatchie, and the thousand other little items of note, the minutiae which in themselves comparatively insignificant nevertheless were component parts of one grand whole, brilliant in conception, admirable in execution, and gloriously successful beyond the hopes of the most sanguine- the taking of Lookout Mountain and the storming of the heights of Mission Ridge.

The reader of history as he looks on the past is wont to gaze with admiration and reverence on the exploits of the brave heroes of the Pass of Thermopylae, on the Plains of Marathon, in the streets of gory Schernaya; he gazes upon the awful grandeur and brilliant heroism displayed on the fields of Austerlitz and Waterloo and is lost in admiration at those series of successful results, intrepid charges, and the steady valor which culminated in a radiant splendor by the capture of the Halls of the Montezuma. And even in our own war, in this our own fraternal strife, how many deeds of unflinching bravery, how many acts of hardy valor, how many feats of desperate courage have given to history the name and fame of those who accomplished them. But when the history of this war shall be written, when the account of deeds done is rendered up to the God of War, when the balance has been stricken and impartial judgment announced, the storming of Missionary Ridge will stand forth as the grandest, greatest, and most desperate achievement of the present war and one to which other climes and other wars can produce no parallel.

Housed up in the great prison house of Chattanooga, dangerous almost to poke our noses over the breastworks, with our communications constantly threatened, a bold move was necessary and that move has been made. On Monday morning the 21st, we were ordered out with 100 rounds of cartridges per man and two days' rations. The left center became engaged almost immediately, our picket line being in our then front a distance of not more than a half mile. Then came in plain view the Rebel picket line, the picket reserve, a line of rifle pits, scattering woods tolerably thick with underbrush then an open space of a short quarter strewn with branches of trees to impede our progress; right beyond a long line of bouldered embankments with rifle pits and all these obstructions only brings us to the foot of Missionary Ridge. The left and center gained the ground on the 21st after many and very severe encounters up to the open space spoken of with but few casualties in the 1st Ohio, we being the second line- the 5th Kentucky, 41st Ohio, and 93rd Ohio being the principal losers in our brigade.

On the 22nd, a comparative calm ensued and but a few sanguinary skirmishes added their mite of blood to the wide and deep pool already curdling at the ridge's base. The 23rd was the day of military strategy displayed in the capture of Lookout Mountain by the forces on our right by an attack in front and flank, the flankers marching around, the attacking party up. Loud and long boomed the mountain cannon, fiercely screamed the shell from Moccasin Point, incessantly rattled the musketry, even in the damp, dark night, but by the bright light of the morning's sun, not a solitary Rebel stood; not a soldier stood near the key to Chattanooga's position which according to Braxton Bragg's official dispatches to Richmond was 'impregnable to any assault, flank or front.' On the 24th, Sherman's forces were massed on our left and a struggle commenced for a foothold on Missionary Ridge. Slow but sure progress was made by the heroes of Vicksburg and the series of brilliant engagements that preceded its siege and downfall, the rest of the mammoth line dressing up with the left's advance.

Temporary breastworks had been thrown up all along the line and on the 25th, as the golden orb of day shone forth in all its magnificent splendor, two long blue lines stretching from the river on the left around Chattanooga to Lookout Mountain and the river and railroad on our right presented a magnificent spectacle, and their glittering bayonets as they danced in the sunlight looked more as a gorgeous panoramic than an armed host preparing for the work of death and carnage. At twenty minutes past 1 o'clock, a battery volley was fired, the shrill notes of the brigade bugles sounded forward, we dashed over the ramparts and steadily at quick step wound our way through the tangled mass of brush and stumps, over the clearing, and up to the bouldered embankments at the base of the ridge. Here we breathed; here we took a hasty glance towards heaven, breathed the silent prayer, and then riveted our eyes on the summit of the ridge. It was all well so far. We had driven in the pickets, passed over two lines of works, routed the enemy from his fortifications, drove him out of his rifle pits and up the hill where he joined, we knew not how many thousands more of those bent on desperate resistance to our advance-bent on dealing death and destruction to the devoted band below who were now too far advanced to retreat and who neither had the thought of doing so or the inclination. At least twenty pieces of artillery had played upon our one brigade whilst coming over the open space, but the massed dogs of war let loose their wrath, their reserved wrath. The moment or second we attempted the ascent, showers of shell, grape, and canister, solid iron and shrapnel, leaden hail from thousands of small arms sent their death dealing missiles thick and fast into our ranks, but on and up through fire and smoke, on through the iron sleet, up to the summit of the ridge of death, the goal of victory.

Within twenty feet of the Rebel fortifications on the top, there was a pause, a slight rest taken, right over these fortifications, Rebel bullets whistled, Rebels' rifles gleamed. Their batteries were powerless now, they were too near the range of their own men. Their men behind the works dared not show their heads or else a Federal bullet went crashing through their brain. Forward again, over the works, down in the ditches. Away flew the Rebels; after them the Yankees and each one, elated beyond measure at their brilliant success, took his own road after confused Secessia, slaying and maiming, taking prisoners and capturing cannon far after nightfall. Wilder's mounted men started in pursuit on the morning of the 26th and the dull echoes of cannon in the distance shows that he is close on the track of the flying chivalry and Hooker and Sherman who have taken the advance in order to be in at the death, send ever and anon, a leaden pill along the flight towards Atlanta.

The reverse at Chickamauga is retrieved with interest compounded. Sixteen pieces of cannon with an indefinite quantity of small arms are the trophies of our (Hazen's) brigade; also 1,300 prisoners (about 250 of them wounded), three stand of colors, and seven baggage wagons. The 1st Ohio was in Hazen's (2nd) Brigade of Wood's (3rd) Division of Granger's (4th) Corps and as usual maintained its old renown and acquired a bright fame. Our wounded is large, but not so large either when we take into consideration the hazardousness of the enterprise without the aid of either cavalry or artillery. The loss in the 1st Ohio is as follows; many of the wounded will die.

Killed-commissioned officers: 1, Wounded- commissioned officers: 4, Killed-enlisted men: 11, Wounded- enlisted men: 57, Total: 73 Missing-none

Fairfield County can claim her full share in the recent engagements. Gen. Sherman, Col. Moore, Majors Stafford, Butterfield, and Giesy, six companies of the 17th Ohio, two of the 46th Ohio, one of the 52nd Ohio, and one of the 1st Ohio. Color Corporal John Ewing of Co. I was shot down with the colors;[24] Private William W. McLaughlin of Co. I picked them up and was in a short time killed; Corporal Tommy Bowles of Co. A then took the colors and was wounded twice;[25] Capt. Trapp seized them and bore them until he too was wounded and they then passed from another's hands to that of Major Stafford's who, with a squad of about a dozen, charged successfully four times their numbers many times during the evening.

Official reports will give you all the needful particulars to enable you to award honor where honor is due, and I shall close for the present as we have just received marching orders for some place- destination unknown. But three days before the storming of the ridge, Freeman Wolf[26] had been promoted to sergeant, Thomas Bowles, Mathias Dilger, and Milton Hunter to corporals- their good conduct shone none the less conspicuously in battle, a fact fully attested on many a sanguinary field of blood. Henry Bowers[27] is one or was one of the best soldiers in the army and the loss of either the one or the others would be deeply felt in the company (all men mentioned here had been wounded-Ed. Note). God grant we may have no more Missionary Ridges to capture but many more as brilliant victories.

The Lancaster Gazette, December 10, 1863, pg. 2

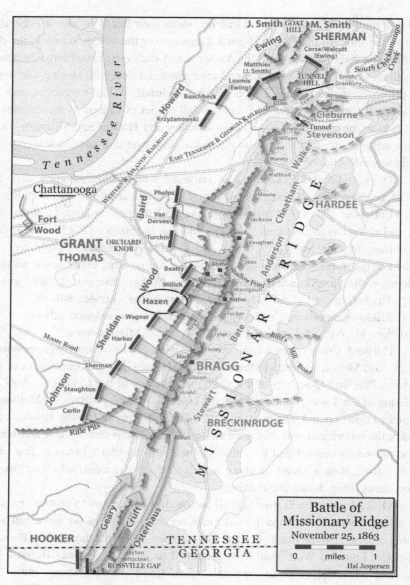

The assault on Missionary Ridge, with Hazen's Brigade (of which the 1st Ohio formed a part) circled near the center of the Union line. The regiment's orders were to storm the rifle pits at the base of the ridge; this was quickly done but the men saw the key to the position was the ridge. Lt. Col. Langdon led his men to the crest, being severely wounded in the face. Five regimental colors bearers were shot down before Major Joab Stafford seized the flag and led the men over the top. Private Comer wrote after the battle "God grant that we have no more Missionary Ridges to capture, but many more as brilliant victories." Map by Hal Jespersen. CWMaps.com

The barren nature of Missionary Ridge that Comer described in his account is evident in this photo taken in late 1863 after the battle. "At twenty minutes past 1 o'clock, a battery volley was fired, the shrill notes of the brigade bugles sounded forward, we dashed over the ramparts and steadily at quick step wound our way through the tangled mass of brush and stumps, over the clearing, and up to the bouldered embankments at the base of the ridge," he wrote. The regiment lost 12 men killed and 66 wounded in their charge upon Missionary Ridge. (Library of Congress)

Official report of Major Joab A. Stafford of the Battle of Missionary Ridge

Camp in the field near Knoxville, Tennessee
December 9, 1863

I have the honor to report the part taken by the 1st Ohio Regiment in the engagements of the 23rd, 24th, and 25th near Chattanooga. On the afternoon of the 23rd, the regiment was consolidated with the 23rd Kentucky under the command of Lt. Col. Langdon of the 1st Ohio and took its position, forming double column, closed in mass on the right and in rear of the front line. In this manner the regiment advanced until the line in front became hotly engaged with the enemy. At this moment I was ordered by Col. Langdon to take two companies from the battalion and move to the right oblique for the purpose of protecting the flank. I did so, taking Co. B, 1st Ohio and one company from the 23rd Kentucky and pressed forward, taking possession of the enemy's line of breastworks on the right, being opposed only by a slim line of skirmishers. A few moments after we had occupied the enemy's works, they appeared upon our extreme right for the purpose no doubt of turning our flank. I deployed a line of skirmishers to cover the flank. At this moment Lt. Col. Langdon came up with the balance of the command, drove the enemy back and held the position. In this skirmish, the regiment behaved nobly, losing one man killed and three wounded.

On the night of the 23rd, the regiment was occupied in strengthening the positions and doing picket duty. Nothing worthy of note happened on the 24th.

About 8 o'clock on the morning of the 25th, two companies of the 1st Ohio being out on the skirmish line were ordered to advance along with the balance of the skirmishers of the brigade. They advanced to within about 300 yards of the enemy's entrenchments under a sharp fire from their infantry and artillery. Soon after the two companies from the 1st Ohio were relieved and rejoined their regiment. Lines were then formed preparatory to an advance upon the enemy's works. The 1st Ohio took position on the right in the front line, deployed-the first line being under command of Lt. Col. Langdon. About 2 o'clock, the line advanced under a heavy fire from the enemy's infantry and artillery. Their first line of works were carried by storm and after a few minutes rest the men pressed steadily forward up Missionary Ridge. About two-thirds the way up, Lt. Col. Langdon fell severely wounded while bravely leading his men forward. The brave Capt. Nicholas Trapp (Co. G) fell about the same time, badly wounded. Still the men moved steadily on under terrible fire to the crest of the hill, driving the enemy out of his fortifications, taking a great many prisoners and two pieces of artillery.

The crest of the hill being gained, our position became very critical, our brigade at that time being the only one on the ridge- the enemy sweeping the ridge at every fire from his cannon on the right. Our men became considerably scattered in their advance up the hill and it was with a great deal of difficulty that any considerable number of any one regiment could be got together. Hastily collecting about 20 men of my own regiment and a few from other regiments, I moved to the right along the crest at a double quick driving the enemy away and capturing their first two pieces of artillery on the right, they retiring over the crest to the left and opening a flanking fire upon us again. I ordered a charge and the enemy was driven from their new position. They now opened four pieces of artillery upon us about 100 yards further to the right, and also formed a line of infantry across the crest for the purpose, doubtless, of driving us from the ridge. I now had about 15 men under Capt. Hooker and about 15 more from different regiments; they all seemed determined not to give one inch though they were opposed by four pieces of cannon and nearly a whole regiment of infantry. I gave the command 'forward' and they all started at the double-quick! It seems incredible, nevertheless it is true, our 30 men went at them with a right good will and the enemy broke and scattered in every direction, leaving their four guns and a great number of prisoners in our hands. This last battery was captured immediately in front of Gen. Sheridan's left brigade, they being about one-half way up the ridge. We followed the enemy up, drove them from several pieces of artillery and caissons they were trying to get away. We also captured one cannon, one caisson, and one wagon on the opposite crest of the hill. I then returned and joined my battalion now under the command of Lt. Col. James C. Foy of the 23rd Kentucky.

The regiment behaved most nobly, both officers and men. They all took example from our brave and gallant lieutenant colonel who fell before the action was over. They vied with each other in deeds of heroism. I would respectfully recommend for your favorable consideration Captains Nicholas Trapp, Emanuel Hooker, James E. Jones (Co. C), and William L. Patterson (Co. H); Lieutenants George P. Leonard (Co. E), Solomon Homan (Co. A), Alexander Varian (Co. D), George J. Grove (Co. F), Obediah S. Ward (Co. F), Anton Kuhlman (Co. H), and Charles Young (Co. A). Also Dr. Jacob C. Barr. They are all gallant officers and deserve the highest encomiums for their noble conduct. Second Lt. Christopher Wollenhaupt (Co. I), who was killed while gallantly urging his men forward, was a good officer and beloved by all. His loss is severely felt in the regiment. The loss in the 1st Ohio was heavy: one officer and 11 men killed, four officers and 62 men wounded, making the loss of the regiment since the 23rd totaling 82.

Respectfully submitted,
Joab A. Stafford, Major, commanding regt.

1st Ohio Regt., 2nd Brigade, 3rd Division, 4th Corps
Near Knoxville, Tennessee
December 14, 1863

You will be somewhat surprised at receiving from me a communication dated at this place; but the fact of the matter is that on the 28th of last month we started in three columns for the scattered forces of Secessia- Hooker and Thomas after Bragg, Sherman and Granger after Longstreet, and Burnside and Foster after Jones. What the other forces did I don't know, but Sherman and Granger, 'we, us, and co.', caught nobody and we are now here, living on fresh pork, mutton, beef, corncakes, slapjacks, beef soup, honey, molasses, potatoes, etc.; the 'exigencies of the service' requiring us in the absence of salt meat and hard tack to appropriate all digestible articles to our own use. To be sure, some people don't like it, but others do. As a somewhat better account of the Missionary Ridge affair than I could possibly give you is contained in Major Joab A. Stafford's report of the part taken by our regiment in the fight. I shall here append it, promising it was found at brigade headquarters and copied from the official documents there on file and soon to be transmitted.

We have heard of none of wounded boys since started hither- a distance of 170 miles by our roundabout course, but 100 direct. Henry Bowers, Freeman Wolf, and Thomas Bowles were the worst wounded- two of them perhaps mortally. How long we stay here, whither we go and for what purpose, I know not, but all will be well in a few months more.

The Lancaster Gazette, December 31, 1863, pg. 1

Chapter Six

EASTERN TENNESSEE TO ATLANTA

Knoxville, Tennessee
April 4, 1864

Of all the places I have ever seen, this Knoxville-grand citadel of the Switzerland of America- is certainly the most uncouth and vile. Here can be seen, in all their pristine glory and loveliness, the bogus refugee who had fled from his mountain home to escape Secession steel and lead but who in all likelihood never saw 'oppression' except from a northern dungeon. Here, too, is the crippled soldier with an empty coat sleeve, and arm lost in the service; your heart goes out in sympathy with him until you discover the 'sell' and ascertain that the lost arm is strapped closely to his side. Here can be seen soldiers dressed in citizens' clothes' citizens in soldiers' clothes; bawdy women in men's clothes; drunken niggers arm in arm with drunken white loafers, gay and gallant lieutenants and captains promenading in the sparkling brilliance of the noonday sun with America's daughters of African descent, with the aces, duces, and trays (privates, corporals, and sergeants) follow in the wake with longing eyes. Here, too, are gambling hells, where 'three pluck one' is the motto and where four kings and an ace are beaten by two knaves and a sling shot; whiskey shops, where 50 cents per drink, a person can get the delirium tremens, the small pox, and a black eye, all in the course of a half day.

Brothels, such as might become the 'bottomless pit,' are here in thick profusion, where night is turned into day and day into night, where black and white, male and female, mingle together in one loathsome, saddening, heart sickening, chaotic mass of filth and decomposition. Eating houses also abound, where the kitchen, slop barrel, dining room, and ticket office are all in the same room, and an epicurean's eye and tooth can always tell which domestic cooked his meal by the color of the hair in his bean soup. To sum up, Knoxville's insides are in a state of decomposition, and the scums thrown to the surface by internal festerings find a safe lodgment in the many guard houses, bull pens, jails, and prisons with which the city is supplied, where, although grub and bedding are scarce, the lack is more than compensated for by the plentitude of filth and uncleanliness, by rags and tatters, by the most hideous yells and whoopings, by unlimited quantities of the old Egyptian plague-army gray backs of the largest size and caliber.

You wish to know why all this is? Why 'these things pass us like a summer cloud without' the Provost Marshal 'special wonder?' I'll tell you. The majority of the people here are camp followers, knucks, cracksmen, shoulder hitters, confidence men, etc., who, blended together with the army play offs who possumed sick when their commands left for the front constitute one of the most God-forsaken, law-defying, conglomerated masses of vice and immorality that Heaven in its mercy ever permitted to exist. Turn we now to the other side of the picture-Hyperion to a Satyr!

Brownlow's *Whig and Rebel Ventilator* still spreads the gospel according to the sainted Parson's doctrine, viz; that the road to hell is paved with Rebel bones and that none can enter heaven except Union men. The rooms of the Christian Commission and Sanitary Store are doing their work of love in an appropriate manner and many a hearty 'God bless you' goes up for the unknown donor, who in the distant north knows not the full merit of the charitable donation. Religious exercises are conducted by four different denominations- Methodists, Baptists, Episcopalians, and Roman Catholics. Their influence is at last being felt, and a better grade of morals will shortly supersede the present deplorable state of affairs.

I have never seen but two streets in the city- Gay and Main-although there is a dozen other avenues, footpaths, traces, trails, and what-nots. All these are jammed and crammed with hardware, dry goods, sutler and military stores- no artisan's or mechanic's shops, none of the true blue Yankee thrift and enterprise which competition engenders. Every person seems to have converted himself into a miniature merchant, and the many placards which meet one's gaze inscribed 'pize and cakes heer' or 'good beer fur sail' show that our old friend Hardy, the sign and ornamental painter, has not imparted his skill to operators here. Photographic galleries in pavilion tents have made their appearance lately in order to supply the demand of soldier boys for semblances to send to 'fair correspondents.' Prices- $6.00 per dozen. In this connection I may mention that George Myers of Lancaster is here with his instrument waiting for suckers. I saw him yesterday looking for a boarding house or hotel with a fair prospect of finding one or the other by the time the war closes.

The Union Serenaders regale the denizens nightly (Sundays excepted) with their Ethiopic delineations, comical burlesques, witty sayings, conundrums, etc. But this may possible come to a close soon as the incompetent surgeon of the post seems to think that persons who can stay up nearly all night giving concerts are well enough to go to the front to their commands. Hazen's brigade is near Rutledge and the rest of the army is scattered from there to Strawberry Plains. I do not anticipate a big fight in this department soon as General Hazen and myself are both absent from the brigade which, in my opinion, will have nothing to do just now but guard the 23rd Corps from harm. Granger's 4th Corps has much less to do since the 9th Corps left for the east.

We are all veterans now, having been in the service nearly three years-active field duty all the time. If that don't make a veteran, what will? Four months from this date, at farthest, and those living will receive their furloughs. Until then, good bye, farewell, adieu, au revoir!

The Lancaster Gazette, April 21, 1864, pg. 1

Kingston, Cass Co., Georgia
June 5, 1864

I would have written you earlier than this but the absence of every part of myself from the front is my sole and only excuse for dereliction of duty. I was with my company and regiment at Tunnel Hill, Buzzard's Roost, Rocky Face Ridge, and Resaca when, considering that the campaign was likely to last day and night for several weeks, I was taken with palpitation of the heart brought on by violent nervous excitement. Shortly afterwards, I became severely wounded in the craw, the effects of which will in all likelihood confine me to a bed in the rear until 'picked up' by the provost guard. At any rate, I am now at Kingston, a little, old, dried-up, seedy town which might have contained in its palmy days 204 inhabitants, but which now is tenanted only by men in the government service, a few half-starved house dogs and several refugee families, who have braved the 'Yankee atrocities' promised them by the chivalry and now enjoy their regular meals at governmental expense. Speaking of refugees reminds me that in all the towns and villages we have passed through since the grand advance of Sherman in the early part of May, not one able-bodied nigger was left behind by the valorous, high-toned representatives of the Confederate dynasties, but in their bondsmen's stead their own starving wives and helpless children! Chivalry evidently has faith in Yankee humanity, or on the other hand, sought to save their most valuable possessions from the invader and therefore saved their 'woolies.'

Our army had gained possession since the grand advance by superior strategetical moves, by hard fighting and sturdy iron will, of the Tunnel Hill fortifications, of Rocky Face Ridge, an elevation 400 feet high, perfectly insurmountable on its two sides and one flank; of Buzzard's Roost where no man than a column by company could march in battle line and where an artificial dike was formed to wash our forces into the mouths of batteries thickly planted; of Dalton, Rome, Adairsville, Calhoun, Resaca, Kingston, Cassville, Cartersville, and Stilesboro, and Col. Henry A. Hambright, 79th Pennsylvania commanding this post, had just received verbal information from the front that we now have possession of Marietta and that the iron horses can go snorting and prancing his way 15 miles further on towards the last ditch of Johnson's army, carrying civilization in the shape of powder and ball to rebellious hosts and hard tack meat, and coffee to the boys in army blue. We now 'occupy, hold, and possess' more of the Confederacy's railroads than them themselves; Dalton is 40 miles south of Chattanooga, Resaca, 61 miles, Cassville, 80 miles, Marietta, 102 miles south- the latter the left of our line, Dallas on our right, making the average distance of our army from Atlanta just 14 miles! We have passed the most easily defended portion of the enemy's country, have crossed the Oostenaula, Catoose, and Etowah rivers, have flanked and stormed the fortifications erected by both nature and art, and now stand ready to strike the death blow to rebellion in this department. For all of which we give thanks and heartfelt praise to the brave men, dead and living, who did the work. Gen. Grant is not exactly here in person, but his 'brains' are, in the person of Gen. W.T. Sherman. As Basil Duke was to John Morgan, so was W.T. Sherman to U.S. Grant-only on a higher scale and more extended field of action.

We have not a clear field almost for siege operations, but what move is on the tap no one can guess, although grapevine dispatches are regaled to the rear hourly and the addenda naturally accumulating thereto. Kingston is at present the base of supplies for the army and here is where the sick and wounded are brought to, preparatory to being sent north. Many car loads have left here and I have seen many familiar faces among the unfortunates. Wood's division of the 4th Corps under Howard has suffered terribly, and Hazen's Brigade of this division more so than any other. What is the aggregated loss during the entire campaign I am unable to state, but the 1st Ohio has lost in killed and wounded up to last accounts 107 officers and men. Of the killed and wounded, four have been wounded before: Lt. Solomon Homan at Shiloh through the right arm; Robert Shannon at Stone River, George Myers at Chattanooga, and Joseph Groff at Mission Ridge.

I have great faith in the final complete success of the Union arms and the utter rout and overthrow of the Rebel armies everywhere, but when the shouts of joy go upwards to heaven for the re-cemented Union and a peace based in a perpetuity, I fear but very few of that old company of 118 men brought out by Major Stafford and Capt. Hooker will be left to tell the tale. On the other hand, it may be possible that no other casualties may occur. So mote it be. Private David Rhodes, properly a member of Co. A but a transfer to Co. D was again wounded near Burnt Hickory-Major Stafford, commanding the regiment, had a ball pass through 52 thicknesses of pasteboard and lodge in his watch! Capt. Nicholas Trapp with but one useful arm (the result of the Mission Ridge battle) has acted throughout as major, refusing his discharge until expiration of service.

The Atlanta railroad has not been destroyed and rations come up punctually to here, from whence they are transported by road to the front in wagons. Sanitary goods come into the hospitals gradually, but the demand of the sick and wounded for something more palatable than army fare overreaches the supply. In this connection I may state that I have ever looked upon sutlers as a necessary evil, a species of humanity to be endured with regret; yet when I saw them taking out canned fruit, apple butter, soft bread, and other delicacies to the maimed and crippled soldiers on the cars, my idea of 'army thieves' changed considerably. Foremost in this work of love and patriotic sympathy was S.B. Bickford and Jack Reed, doing business for W.J. Carty, sutler, 90th O.V.I. A few more men such as these, who supplied to men they had never seen and in all likelihood would never see again would be a blessing to the army, and elevate sutlering to what it was intended to be- a blessing to all.

I have already written more than I intended to in the start. In fact, I do not like my present course of 'Go in boys and clean them out!' It should be, 'Come on boys, let's give them fits!' Phrenologists tell me I have one bump very largely developed. Possibly. From the hips down I am not reliable, but from there up, I am every particle O.K.

The Lancaster Gazette, June 23, 1864, pg. 1

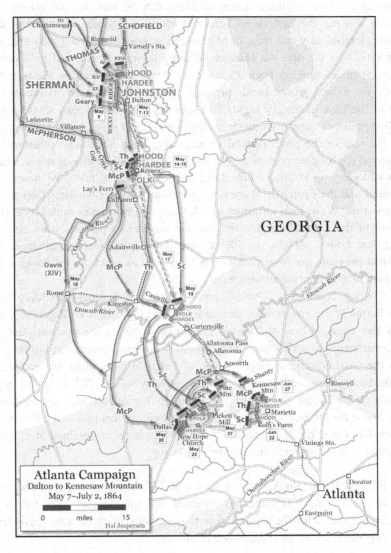

The Atlanta Campaign
Map by Hal Jespersen. CWMaps.com

Chattanooga, Tennessee
August 21, 1864

To one who has not been in Chattanooga for some months past, everything appears strange and unfamiliar. Where, a year since, old rickety tumble down buildings were seen on every side now appear large commodious warehouses and mercantile establishments, where anything and everything can be had for the asking, provided always that you put the cash down before touching the goods. Sutler shops and slush houses are plentiful as wood ticks in Mississippi or gray backs on a duty soldier, where the substantials of life and the luxuries of army tables are supplied to wayfarers and sojourners at prices ranging from 25 cents for a two inch imitation pie to a full sized greenback for a half grown meal- presenting a striking contrast to the eye and the stomach of the time of hungry nights and lean days in Chattanooga where half-starved men pulled grains of corn from under mules' feet, picked up discarded soup bones from offal in the rear of the governmental commissary. Then no hotel, restaurant, or lunch house greeted the longing eyes of those 'sons of Mars' who shortly after moving away to hardtack and glory up Mission Ridge and Lookout Mountain; now two mammoth hotels (The Central and the Crutchfield) are open and doing a better business than any hotel of Cincinnati or the West. I am informed by a fat corporal who takes in tickets at the dining room door of the Crutchfield that the average number of persons who have taken of meals at that house per day is 500 at one dollar per meal in advance. This last arrangement prevents me from patronizing the house as much as I otherwise should in case no such preparatory installment were demanded.

Charley Kutz, A.L. Clark, Abner White, and Samuel McCleery each have lucrative berths in the government service here. Ex-Lt. William H. Pugh, now on a visit home, is also engaged here and all are spoken of as giving the best satisfaction in the several departments to which they are attached. A deserved promotion has recently been made in the Quartermaster's Dept. of one of Fairfield's favorites, the recipient of the promotion being Capt. Augustus R. Keller, formerly of the 90th Ohio. In addition to performing faithfully all the duties pertaining to his office, the captain keeps open boarding house for his Fairfield friends and in this city of dirt pies and hair soup, a clean square meal as Capt. Keller's hospitality affords is not to be obtained at all times. The *Chattanooga Gazette* this morning has the following:

Promoted: Captain A.R. Keller of the 90th Ohio, for more than a year A.A.Q.M. of the Engineer Brigade has received the appointment of a full A.Q.M. in accordance with the earnest recommendations of those who have learned to appreciate an active and competent officer.

This gives the captain all the perquisites and advantages of a staff officer and makes his position a permanency and not a detachment. None more fully deserve it.

Five companies of the 1st Ohio have gone home and one more will be in the city for mustering out today. The non-veterans of the 17th, 43rd, 46th, and 30th, in all of which Fairfield is represented, will be home the last of this month. We suppose no question will arise as to our right to vote at the next election. When your humble correspondent will be home is not known to anyone at the present writing, but it will not be long after I get permission to do so.

Nothing has transpired of a military character in this city since I have been here, with the exception of the arming and sending of all soldiers except patrol guards in order to crush the further operations of the Rebel raider General Wheeler. Part of the force sent out was the 14th and 16th U.S.C.T., vulgarly called 'nigger regiments.' How they acted or what they did I do not know, but one thing is certain: they are well drilled and well disciplined. I was an eye witness to one of their dress parades and shall go and see the sight again whenever convenient. There they stood, as immovable as statues, white kid gloves on their delicate hands, heels together, bodies thrown slightly forward, little fingers of the left hands on the seams of their breecherloons, eyes square to the front when the command 'on the center dress' was given. Two strokes of lightning coming from opposite directions and meeting together at a given point will be a simile for their whites of the eyes that sent their electric flash towards the stars and stripes of the U.S.C.T. at the word of execution.

During the scare here, all drinking houses were closed and that in Chattanooga means a great deal. At such time when everybody is sober, no fist fights occur, no pockets are picked, no railroad accidents happen, no confidence games are played on the unsuspecting, no breakdowns from carelessness of drivers occurs. In short, the city is a 'dead mackerel in the sun' but is all the better for morality and virtue. Persons visiting Chattanooga will find me for a few days yet somewhere near the Soldier's Home when I am out of money; but if flush I can be found at all times in close proximity to the dining room of the Crutchfield.

The Lancaster Gazette, September 1, 1864, pg. 3

Company Rosters

COMPANY A, 1ST OHIO VOLUNTEER INFANTRY, NINETY DAYS' SERVICE
"Lancaster Guards"

Mustered into service at Lancaster, Pennsylvania April 29, 1861 by Alexander McD. McCook, First Lieutenant, 3rd Infantry, U.S.A., mustering officer. Mustered out August 3, 1861 at Columbus, Ohio by Howard Hanshaw, Captain, Topographical Engineers, U.S.A., mustering officer.

Name	Rank	In	Out	Notes
Stafford, Joab A.	CAPT	April 16, 1861	August 3, 1861	
Hunter, Thomas M.	1LT	April 16, 1861	August 3, 1861	
Ricketts, Ezra	2lT	April 16, 1861	August 3, 1861	
Butterfield, Benj. F.	SGT	April 16, 1861	August 3, 1861	
O'Harra, Hugh	SGT	April 17, 1861	August 3, 1861	
Borland, Charles	SGT	April 16, 1861	August 3, 1861	
Weakley, James T.	SGT	April 16, 1861	August 3, 1861	
Butterfield, Isaac	CPL	April 16, 1861	August 3, 1861	
Heed, Charles	CPL	April 16, 1861	August 3, 1861	
Sullivan, Daniel	CPL	April 16, 1861	August 3, 1861	
Fetters, Albert	CPL	April 16, 1861	August 3, 1861	
Mytinger, James	MUSC	April 16, 1861	August 3, 1861	
Jeffries, Ambrose	MUSC	April 16, 1861	August 3, 1861	
Arehart, John	PVT	April 16, 1861	August 3, 1861	
Arney, Milton	PVT	April 16, 1861	August 3, 1861	
Baggott, Charles	PVT	April 16, 1861	August 3, 1861	
Ball, Henry	PVT	April 16, 1861	August 3, 1861	
Barnes, Leroy	PVT	April 16, 1861	August 3, 1861	
Barnes, Lyman	PVT	April 16, 1861	August 3, 1861	
Benadum, Peter	PVT	April 16, 1861	August 3, 1861	
Brenner, John	PVT	April 16, 1861	August 3, 1861	
Brown, William	PVT	April 16, 1861	August 3, 1861	
Church, Robert	PVT	April 16, 1861	August 3, 1861	
Clark, William	PVT	April 16, 1861	August 3, 1861	
Comer, Harrison	PVT	April 16, 1861	August 3, 1861	
Cornwell, Levi	PVT	April 16, 1861	August 3, 1861	
Cutchaw, James	PVT	April 16, 1861	June 25, 1861	Disch. for disability
Daughtery, Hugh	PVT	April 16, 1861	August 3, 1861	
Denton, Mathias	PVT	April 16, 1861	August 3, 1861	
Dittmer, Jacob	PVT	April 16, 1861	August 3, 1861	
Elder, Samuel	PVT	April 16, 1861	August 3, 1861	
Engle, Samuel	PVT	April 16, 1861	August 3, 1861	
Ewing, Robert S.	PVT	April 16, 1861	August 3, 1861	
Feighley, William	PVT	April 16, 1861	August 3, 1861	
Field, Charles	PVT	April 16, 1861	August 3, 1861	
Flemm, Joseph	PVT	April 16, 1861	August 3, 1861	
Getz, Henry	PVT	April 16, 1861	August 3, 1861	
Gordon, James	PVT	April 16, 1861	August 3, 1861	

Name	Rank	In	Out	Notes
Guseman, John	PVT	April 16, 1861	August 3, 1861	
Hafler, Joseph	PVT	April 16, 1861	August 3, 1861	
Ham, Edward	PVT	April 16, 1861	August 3, 1861	
Holtzman, Henry	PVT	April 16, 1861	August 3, 1861	
Holtzman, Reese	PVT	April 16, 1861	August 3, 1861	
Hoover, John	PVT	April 16, 1861	August 3, 1861	
Jones, Daniel	PVT	April 16, 1861	August 3, 1861	
Keller, James	PVT	April 16, 1861	August 3, 1861	
Larinser, James E.	PVT	April 16, 1861	August 3, 1861	
Linn, Christian	PVT	April 16, 1861	August 3, 1861	
Lochner, William	PVT	April 16, 1861	August 3, 1861	
Lockary, Daniel	PVT	April 16, 1861	August 3, 1861	
McClain, James	PVT	April 16, 1861	August 3, 1861	
McClure, Andrew	PVT	April 16, 1861	August 3, 1861	
Michaels, George W.	PVT	April 16, 1861	August 3, 1861	
Michaels, William H.	PVT	April 16, 1861	August 3, 1861	
Mutchler, Amos	PVT	April 16, 1861	August 3, 1861	
Nichols, Asa	PVT	April 16, 1861	August 3, 1861	
Oare, Charles	PVT	April 16, 1861	August 3, 1861	
Poulton, Minor R.	PVT	April 16, 1861	August 3, 1861	
Rapp, John	PVT	April 16, 1861	August 3, 1861	
Reece, John C.	PVT	April 16, 1861	August 3, 1861	
Richard, William	PVT	April 16, 1861	August 3, 1861	
Scott, Harvey	PVT	April 16, 1861	August 3, 1861	
Shannon, Robert	PVT	April 16, 1861	August 3, 1861	
Shook, Jacob	PVT	April 16, 1861	August 3, 1861	
Showers, Benjamin	PVT	April 16, 1861	August 3, 1861	
Shrieves, Thomas	PVT	April 16, 1861	August 3, 1861	
Sleicher, Philip	PVT	April 16, 1861	August 3, 1861	
Stermer, Peter	PVT	April 16, 1861	August 3, 1861	
Strentz, Charles	PVT	April 16, 1861	August 3, 1861	
Swigert, William	PVT	April 16, 1861	June 18, 1862	POW July 21, 1861 at Bull Run; Disch.at Ft.Columbus, N.Y. Harbor
Titler, Harrison	PVT	April 16, 1861	August 3, 1861	
Tobin, Elijah	PVT	April 16, 1861	August 3, 1861	
Walters, Henry	PVT	April 16, 1861	August 3, 1861	
Weeks, Jesse J.	PVT	April 16, 1861	August 3, 1861	
Winchester, Charles	PVT	April 16, 1861	August 3, 1861	
Willi, David	PVT	April 16, 1861	August 3, 1861	
Wolf, Newton J.	PVT	April 16, 1861	August 3, 1861	
Wyman, George W.	PVT	April 16, 1861	August 3, 1861	

COMPANY A, 1ST OHIO VOLUNTEER INFANTRY, THREE YEARS' SERVICE

"Lancaster Guards"

Mustered into service October 5, 1861 at Camp Corwin, Dayton, Ohio;
Mustered out of service August 15, 1864 at Chattanooga, Tennessee

Name	Rank	In	Out	Notes
Stafford, Joab A.	CAPT	August 1, 1861	June 2, 1862	Promoted to MAJ
Hooker, Emanuel T.	CAPT	August 1, 1861	August 15, 1864	Promoted from 1LT June 2, 1862
Wiley, James M.	1LT	August 1, 1861	December 23, 1862	Promoted from 2LT June 2, 1862
Homan, Solomon	1LT	August 1, 1861	August 15, 1864	Promoted from 1SGT to 2LT January 2, 1863; promoted to 1LT May 5, 1863
Leonard, George P.	2LT	August 20, 1861	May 12, 1863	Promoted from SGMJ June 2, 1862; promoted to 1LT January 3, 1863; assigned to Company E May 12, 1863
Young, Charles	2LT	August 1, 1861	June 12, 1864	Promoted from SGT August 26, 1863; discharged on a surgeon's certificate of disability
Timmons, Samuel P.	1SGT	August 1, 1861	September 16, 1864	Appointed SGT from PVT October 26, 1862; appointed 1SGT December 23, 1862; wounded and captured September 19, 1863 at the Battle of Chickamauga; died at Andersonville Prison Camp September1 6, 1864
Ross, William	SGT	August 1, 1861	August 15, 1864	Appointed SGT from CPL December 23, 1862
Pomfret, Henry	SGT	August 17, 1861	?	Appointed CPL October 20, 1862; promoted to SGT November 2, 1863; wounded July 21, 1864 near Atlanta; no further record
Dilger, Mathias L.	SGT	August 18, 1861	August 15, 1864	Appointed CPL November 2, 1863; promoted to SGT May 1, 1864
Applegate, Walter	SGT	August 1, 1861	May 15, 1864	Promoted to SGT from CPL October 26, 1862; killed in action May 15, 1864 at the Battle of Resaca
Holtzman, John R.	SGT	August 7, 1861	February 16, 1862	Died of disease at Louisville, KY
Murphy, James	SGT	August 1, 1861	July 10, 1864	Appointed CPL August 1, 1863; promoted to SGT March 1, 1864; died July 10, 1864 of wounds sustained July 9, 1864 at the Battle of Chattahoochee Bridge
Wolf, Freeman M.	SGT	August 21, 1861	December 5, 1863	Appointed CPL June 12, 1863; promoted to SGT November 2, 1863; died December 5, 1863 of wounds received November 25, 1863 in the Battle of Mission Ridge
Shannon, Robert	CPL	August 10, 1861	August 15, 1864	
Porter, Noble C.	CPL	August 8, 1861	August 15, 1864	Appointed CPL Oct. 20, 1862
Hunter, Milton	CPL	August 18, 1861	August 15, 1864	Appointed CPL Nov. 2, 1863
Brown, John L.	CPL	August 1, 1861	August 15, 1864	Appointed CPL May 1, 1864
Carroll, George W.	CPL	August 1, 1861	August 15, 1864	Appointed CPL May 1, 1864
Heberly, William	CPL	August 1, 1861	June 15, 1864	Appointed CPL February 12, 1863; died June 15, 1864 of wounds received May 27, 1864 in the battle near Acworth, Georgia
Bowles, Thomas	CPL	August 10, 1861	June 6, 1864	Appointed CPL Nov. 2, 1863; wounded November 25, 1863 at the Battle of Mission Ridge; discharged June 6, 1864 on a surgeon's certificate of disability for wounds received
Lewis, Solomon B.	CPL	August 1, 1861	October 2, 1862	Disch. for disability at Columbus
Asbell, Sylvester	PVT	August 1, 1861	January 7, 1863	Died of disease at Nashville, TN
Allen, George W.	PVT	August 1, 1861	October 2, 1862	Disch. for disability
Bagley, Spencer	PVT	August 1, 1861	October 15, 1863	Enlisted in regular army
Baker, Thomas	PVT	September 20, 1861	August 15, 1864	

Name	Rank	In	Out	Notes
Barrett, John F.	PVT	September 5, 1861	?	Transf. to Invalid Corps
Barrett, Samuel T.	PVT	September 5, 1861	August 15, 1864	
Bennett, James W.	PVT	August 30, 1861	July 2, 1863	Killed by accidental discharge of shell July 2, 1863 at Tullahoma, TN
Bessinger, Henry	PVT	August 1, 1861	August 15, 1864	
Bowers, Henry	PVT	August 10, 1861	November 26, 1863	Died of wounds sustained Nov. 25, 1863 at the Battle of Mission Ridge
Bretz, Adolphus	PVT	August 1, 1861	August 15, 1864	
Brown, John F.	PVT	September 1, 1861	August 15, 1864	
Carlis, William	PVT	August 1, 1861	August 15, 1864	
Cassell, William	PVT	August 21, 1861	August 15, 1864	
Cloud, William	PVT	August 1, 1861	October 12, 1861	Transf. to Co. D
Cly, Theodore	PVT	August 21, 1861	October 12, 1861	Transf. to Co. D
Coffman, Benj. F.	PVT	August 21, 1861	August 15, 1864	
Colwell, James	PVT	August 21, 1861	January 31, 1862	Died at Woodsonville, KY
Comer, Harry	PVT	August 18, 1861	May 1, 1863	Transf. to Co. I
Copeland, Caleb	PVT	August 1, 1861	April 10, 1864	Wounded and captured Sept. 19, 1863 at the Battle of Chickamauga; died at Andersonville Prison Camp April 10, 1864
Deaver, Tilman	PVT	August 25, 1863	October 7, 1863	Draftee; died at Chattanooga
Deeds, Benjamin G.	PVT	August 8, 1863	November 16, 1863	Draftee; died at Chattanooga
Deeds, Jacob D.	PVT	August 8, 1863	June 30, 1864	Draftee; discharged at expiration of nine months' service.
Deitz, Henry	PVT	August 1, 1861	June 24, 1864	Died June 24, 1864 at Chattanooga of wounds received May 27, 1864 in action near Acworth, GA
Dennis, Jeremiah	PVT	August 21, 1861	?	Transf. to Invalid Corps
Denton, Henry W.	PVT	August 1, 1861	August 15, 1864	
Evans, Charles C.	PVT	August 21, 1861	March 5, 1862	Disch. for disability
Flemm, Joseph C.	PVT	August 21, 1861	October 12, 1861	Transf. to Co. D
Fricker, George	PVT	August 21, 1861	August 15, 1864	
Frizzell, Frederick	PVT	August 21, 1861	May 2, 1864	Absent, sick in hospital in St. Louis, MO since April 27, 1862; mustered out by order of War Dept.
Galbreath, Benjamin	PVT	September 15, 1863	June 30, 1864	Draftee; disch at expiration of nine month's service.
Gardner, William A.	PVT	August 8, 1863	June 30, 1864	Draftee; disch. at expiration of nine months' service.
Glarrsee, Isaac D.	PVT	August 8, 1861	August 15, 1864	
Grandlienard, Chas.	PVT	August 1, 1861	?	Wounded and captured September 19, 1863 at the Battle of Chickamauga; no further record
Griffith, George	PVT	August 12, 1861	August 16, 1862	Disch. for disability
Groff, Ignatius	PVT	August 1, 1861	August 15, 1864	
Groff, Joseph	PVT	August 10, 1861	May 27, 1864	Killed in action near Acworth, GA
Haraman, William H.	PVT	August 8, 1863	June 30, 1864	Draftee; disch at expiration of nine month's service.
Harney, Charles	PVT	August 18, 1861	August 15, 1864	
Harman, William E.	PVT	August 8, 1861	August 15, 1864	
Hartman, Ethan	PVT	August 10, 1861	January 30, 1864	Died at Knoxville, TN
Hartman, William F.	PVT	August 14, 1863	June 30, 1864	Draftee; disch at expiration of nine month's service.

Name	Rank	In	Out	Notes
Harvey, William H.	PVT	August 12, 1861	December 30, 1863	Transf. to Invalid Corps
Hasson, Jacob K.	PVT	August 8, 1861	August 15, 1864	
Heberly, John	PVT	August 1, 1861	August 15, 1864	
Heist, Thomas	PVT	August 1, 1861	March 1, 1864	Died at Lancaster, OH
Hunter, Solomon	PVT	August 12, 1861	?	Disch. for disability
Johnston, William R.	PVT	August 1, 1861	May 10, 1862	Disch. for disability
Lardin, William	PVT	August 21, 1861	August 15, 1864	
Laws, James	PVT	August 1, 1861	December 12, 1862	Disch. for disability
Lewis, James	PVT	August 18, 1861	February 10, 1863	Disch. for disability
Lewis, Jesse	PVT	August 9, 1861	April 10, 1863	Captured December 31, 1862 at

the Battle of Stones River; disch for disability April 10, 1863; died of disease April 13, 1863 at Camp Parole, Annapolis, MD

Name	Rank	In	Out	Notes
Lewis, Noah F.	PVT	September 15, 1861	1864	Wounded in action May 27, 1864

near Acworth, GA; absent at company mustering out

Name	Rank	In	Out	Notes
Manler, John H.	PVT	August 1, 1861	August 15, 1864	
Martin, Robert	PVT	August 25, 1863	May 28, 1864	Draftee; disch. on expiration of

nine months' service.

Name	Rank	In	Out	Notes
Mason, Isaac	PVT	August 15, 1861	August 19, 1862	Disch. for disability
Matthias, Levi	PVT	August 1, 1861	August 15, 1864	
McCarthy, John	PVT	August 1, 1861	September 24, 1863	Killed in action September 24,

1863 near Chattanooga, TN

Name	Rank	In	Out	Notes
McGill, James	PVT	August 20, 1861	January 10, 1865	Wounded and captured

September 19, 1863 at the Battle of Chickamauga; disch. on expiration of service

Name	Rank	In	Out	Notes
McMullen, Thomas	PVT	August 1, 1861	August 15, 1864	
Miller, John	PVT	August 8, 1861	August 15, 1864	
Moore, Jacob	PVT	August 18, 1861	June 1, 1862	Died of disease at Louisville, KY
Morris, William	PVT	August 1, 1861	?	
Mosier, Augustus M.	PVT	August 20, 1861	?	Disch. for disability
Murphy, David	PVT	August 1, 1861	November 24, 1862	Died of disease at Louisville, KY
Myers, George M.	PVT	August 16, 1861	August 15, 1864	
Parker, Wilson	PVT	August 18, 1863	?	Draftee; wounded September 19,

1863 at the Battle of Chickamauga; no further record

Name	Rank	In	Out	Notes
Peck, John	PVT	August 18, 1861	October 12, 1861	Transf. to Co. D
Peterson, Jeremiah	PVT	August 1, 1861	October 12, 1861	Transf. to Co. D
Poulton, Minor R.	PVT	August 10, 1861	July 9, 1864	Killed in action July 9, 1864 at

the Battle of Chattahoochee Bridge, GA

Name	Rank	In	Out	Notes
Reber, Benjamin	PVT	August 17, 1861	May 28, 1862	Died near Corinth, MS
Rebomer, Allen	PVT	August 15, 1861	?	Absent in hospital at Madison,

IN since October 2, 1863 at company muster out

Name	Rank	In	Out	Notes
Reed, Benjamin	PVT	August 31, 1863	September 19, 1863	Draftee; killed in action

September 19, 1863 at the Battle of Chickamauga

Name	Rank	In	Out	Notes
Reed, John W.	PVT	August 10, 1861	April 30, 1863	Disch. for disability
Road, David	PVT	August 17, 1861	October 12, 1861	Transf. to Co. D
Rockey, William H.	PVT	August 1, 1861	?	Captured December 31, 1862 at

the Battle of Stones River; wounded in action June 17, 1864 near Kennesaw Mtn. GA; absent in hospital at company mustering out

Name	Rank	In	Out	Notes
Saylor, George W.	PVT	August 12, 1861	October 12, 1861	Transf. to Co. D
Schermerhorn, Jas.	PVT	August 1, 1861	February 2, 1862	Disch. for disability

Name	Rank	In	Out	Notes
Schopp, Martin	PVT	August 17, 1861	April 30, 1862	Wounded April 7, 1862 at the Battle of Shiloh; died of wounds April 30, 1862 on steamboat near Evansville, IN
Shannon, John	PVT	August 25, 1861	August 15, 1864	
Shetzley, William	PVT	August 21, 1861	?	Transf. to Invalid Corps
Shook, Jacob	PVT	August 21, 1861	February 9, 1863	Disch. by order of War Dept.
Smith, Aaron S.	PVT	August 1, 1861	August 15, 1864	
Smith, Amos	PVT	August 1, 1861	August 15, 1864	
Smith, Christopher F.	PVT	August 1, 1861	February 12, 1862	Disch. for disability
Smith, James	PVT	August 1, 1861	August 15, 1864	
Smith, Nathan M.	PVT	August 1, 1861	?	Wounded in action May 24, 1864; absent in hospital at company mustering out
Sorgil, Earhart	PVT	August 14, 1863	?	Draftee; wounded September 19, 1863 at the Battle of Chickamauga; absent in hospital
Stamets, Cyrus	PVT	August 27, 1863	June 30, 1864	Draftee; disch. on expiration of nine month's service
Stober, Edward	PVT	August 1, 1861	January 25, 1865	Wounded and captured September 19, 1863 at the Battle of Chickamauga; disch. on expiration of term of service.
Stoneburner, Eli	PVT	August 21, 1861	?	Disch. by order of War Dept.
Stuart, Hiram	PVT	August 18, 1863	June 30, 1864	Draftee; disch. on expiration of nine months' service
Stutzman, Levi	PVT	August 21, 1861	April 29, 1863	Disch. for disability
Thornberry, Edward	PVT	August 21, 1861	?	Wounded July 9, 1864 at the Battle of Chattahoochee Bridge; absent in hospital at company mustering out
Wagner, Levi	PVT	August 21, 1861	?	Wounded May 27, 1864 in action near Acworth, GA; absent in hospital at company mustering out
Webb, Nimrod	PVT	August 1, 1861	January 11, 1863	Died of wounds sustained December 31, 1862 at the Battle of Stones River
Williams, Grafton	PVT	October 1, 1862	October 5, 1864	Draftee; joined company August 11, 1863; wounded November 25, 1863 at the Battle of Mission Ridge; disch. on expiration of term of service
Williams, Henry	PVT	August 2, 1861	?	
Willison, Riley	PVT	August 21, 1861	August 15, 1864	
Wills, David M.D.	PVT	August 10, 1861	March 15, 1863	Enlisted in the regular army
Wisner, Henry S.	PVT	August 25, 1863	August 15, 1864	Draftee; mustered out with company
Zebold, Andrew	PVT	September 8, 1861	August 15, 1864	
Zebold, George	PVT	August 1, 1861	August 15, 1864	

Civil War Service of the 1st Ohio Volunteer Infantry

BULL RUN TO ATLANTA

Ninety Days' Service

Organized at large April 14 to April 29, 1861. Mustered in April 17, 1861. Moved to Washington, D.C., April 19, and duty in the Defenses of that city till July. Attached to Schenck's Brigade, Tyler's Division, McDowell's Army of Northeast Virginia. Actions at Vienna, Va., June 17 and July 9. McDowell's advance on Manassas, Va., July 16-21. Occupation of Fairfax Court House, Va., July 17. Battle of Bull Run, Va., July 21. Cover retreat to Washington. Ordered to Ohio and mustered out August 2, 1861, expiration of term.

Three Years' Service

Organized at Camp Corwin, Dayton, Ohio, August 5 to October 30, 1861.

Moved to Cincinnati, Ohio, October 31; thence to Louisville, Ky., November 5, and to West Point, Ky., November 8. Moved to Elizabethtown and Camp Nevin, Ky., November 15-16. Camp at Bacon Creek and Green River, Ky., till February, 1862.

Attached to 4th Brigade, 2nd Division, Army of Ohio, to September, 1862. 4th Brigade, 2nd Division, 1st Army Corps, Army of Ohio, to November, 1862. 3rd Brigade, 2nd Division, Right Wing 14th Army Corps, Army of the Cumberland, to January, 1863. 3rd Brigade, 2nd Division, 20th Army Corps, Army of the Cumberland, to October, 1863. 2nd Brigade, 3rd Division, 4th Army Corps, Army of the Cumberland, to September, 1864.

SERVICE.--March to Nashville, Tenn., February 14-25, 1862. Occupation of Nashville February 25 to March 16. March to Duck River March 16-21, and to Savannah, Tenn., March 31-April 6. Battle of Shiloh, Tenn., April 6-7. Advance on and siege of Corinth, Miss.. April 29-May 30. Duty at Corinth till June 10. Moved to Iuka, Miss., thence to Tuscumbia, Florence and Huntsville, Ala., June 10-July 5. Duty at Boulay Fork till August 30. Expedition to Tullahoma July 14-18. March to Pelham August 24, thence to Altamont August 28. Reconnaissance toward Sequatchie Valley August 29-30. March to Louisville, Ky., in pursuit of Bragg August 30-September 26. Pursuit of Bragg into Kentucky October 1-17. Lawrenceburg October 8. Dog Walk, Perryville, October 9. March to Nashville, Tenn., October 17-November 7, and duty there till December 26. Kimbrough's Mills, Mill Creek, December 6. Advance on Murfreesboro December 26-30. Battle of Stone's River December 30-31, 1862, and January 1-3, 1863. Duty at Murfreesboro till June. Middle Tennessee (or Tullahoma) Campaign June 23-July 7.

Liberty Gap June 24-27. Occupation of Middle Tennessee till August 16. Passage of the Cumberland Mountains and Tennessee River and Chickamauga (Ga.) Campaign August 16- September 22. Battle of Chickamauga September 19-20. Siege of Chattanooga, Tenn., September 24-October 27. Reopening Tennessee River October 26-29. Brown's Ferry October 27. Chattanooga-Ringgold Campaign November 23-27. Orchard Knob November 23. Mission Ridge November 24-25. March to relief of Knoxville November 28-December 8. East Tennessee Campaign December, 1863- January, 1864. Operations about Dandridge January 16-17, 1864. Operations in East Tennessee till April. Atlanta (Ga.) Campaign May 1 to July 25. Demonstration on Rocky Face Ridge and Dalton May 8-13. Battle of Resaca May 14-15. Adairsville May 17. Near Kingston May 18-19. Near Cassville May 19. Advance on Dallas May 22-25. Operations on line of Pumpkin Vine Creek and battles about Dallas, New Hope Church and Allatoona Hills May 25-June 5. Operations about Marietta and against Kennesaw Mountain June 10-July 2. Pine Hill June 11-14. Lost Mountain June 15-17. Assault on Kennesaw June 27. Ruff's Station July 4. Chattahoochee River July 5-17. Chattahoochee Bridge July 9. Peach Tree Creek July 19-20. Siege of Atlanta July 22-26. Ordered to the rear for muster out. Scout from Whitesides, Tenn., to Sulphur Springs September 2-5 (Detachment). Mustered out August 15, 1864 to October 14, 1864. Recruits transferred to 18th Ohio Volunteers Infantry October 31, 1864.

History of the 1ˢᵗ Ohio Volunteer Infantry from Whitelaw Reid's Ohio in the War

The 1ˢᵗ Ohio was organized under President Lincoln's first call for troops in April 1861. Its nucleus was found in some of the old militia companies and it ranks were largely filled by young men of the best social and pecuniary advantages from southwestern Ohio. So prompt was its response to the cry of danger from the capital that within 60 hours after the telegraph that brought the President's call, the cars were bearing the regiment to Washington. It met, however, with vexatious delays on the route and did not arrive on the Potomac till the danger was averted. Its earliest action was that at Vienna, whither General Schenk's brigade, to which it was attached, in careful obedience to General Winfield Scott's orders and with his approval, was moving by rail. The Rebels were found much sooner than General Scott had expected. They fired into the train; but the 1ˢᵗ Ohio followed by the rest of the brigade, hastily debarked, formed on the side of the track, and made so handsome a resistance, that they were presently able to retire unmolested and with comparatively small loss. In the battle of Bull Run, the 1ˢᵗ Ohio had little active share, but it and the rest of the brigade were kept in excellent order through all the disaster and they rendered incalculable service in covering the retreat. Its losses were slight. The term of service of the regiment having now expired, it was sent home and mustered out.

In August 1861, the regiment began to be reorganized for three years' service but the reorganization was not completed until October. Its place of rendezvous was at

Camp Corwin near Dayton. On October 31st, it left Dayton and reached Cincinnati; on November 4th, the regiment received its arms and on 5th left on the steamer *Telegraph No. 3* for Louisville. Arriving at midnight, it went into Camp York near that city. On the 8th of November, at half past one P.M., it embarked for West Point at the mouth of the Salt River. On the 15th of November, the regiment marched via Elizabethtown reaching Camp Nevin on the 16th where it reported to Gen. Alexander McD. McCook, then in command of the Second Division of the Army of the Cumberland. Soon after it was brigaded with the 1st Kentucky or Louisville Legion, 6th Indiana, 1st Battalion of the 15th U.S. Infantry, and battalions of the 16th and 19th U.S. Infantry regiments, forming the Fourth Brigade of the Second Division. On December 9, the regiment marched to Bacon Creek and on the 17th to Green River. During the last four miles, the march was made under the inspiration of music from Willich's guns at Munfordsville. As the regiment marched into camp that evening, the dead and wounded of the 32nd Indiana were being brought in from the field.

It remained in camp at Green River from December 17, 1861-February 14, 1862, during which time it was thoroughly drilled and prepared for the field. On the morning of the 14th, orders were received for the troops to march to West Point, Kentucky, there to take steamers and join the forces under Gen. Grant moving on Fort Henry. Reaching Upton Station, the regiment bivouacked in the snow until the morning of the 16th when news was received of the fall of Fort Henry. This intelligence caused a retrograde movement to Green River. On February 17th, the regiment began its march to Nashville, arriving on March 3, 1862. It went into camp late at night five miles out on the Franklin Turnpike. This march at night will long be remembered for it was pitch dark and rain, snow, and sleet were falling thick and fast. The men had neither tents, blankets, nor shelter of any kind and encamping in an open field on the icy ground, they suffered terribly.

On the 16th of March, the regiment marched with its division to Duck River, opposite Columbia, reaching there on the 21st. Awaiting the completion of a bridge over Duck River, it went into camp. It crossed Duck River on March 31st, and moved toward Savannah. At half past nine A.M. on April 6th, heavy cannonading was heard in the direction of Shiloh which caused a double quick movement forward. The troops marched 13 miles from half past one to half past four P.M., and arrived at Savannah at half past seven P.M. and at Pittsburg Landing at daylight the next morning.

At six A.M., the regiment moved to the front and formed in line of battle, occupying a position on the left of its brigade and to the right of Gen. Crittenden's division. After fighting until about noon, charging and driving the enemy steadily, and recapturing General McClernand's headquarters camp, the regiment retired to replenish its ammunition boxes, leaving a part of the Fifth Brigade as its relief. Ammunition being procured, the 1st Ohio returned to the field and participated in the general charge on the enemy's lines. Gen. Gibson's brigade being menaced by the enemy on its left flank, the 1st Ohio and 19th U.S. went to its relief, arriving just in time to repulse a vigorous attack from the Rebels. This closed the terrible battle. The 1st Ohio was commanded by Col.

B.F. Smith, a regular army officer, whose soldierly qualities and experience undoubtedly saved the regiment from great loss. Other regiments occupying the same position suffered terribly. Its loss in this battle was sixty men and officers killed and wounded. It was ordered back to the landing where it bivouacked that night in the rain and mud.

The regiment participated in the tedious movement on Corinth, having occasional skirmishes. On the 27th of May, six companies of the regiment under Major Bassett Langdon had a brisk fight at Bridge Creek. The enemy's pickets were driven in and the ground held. On the 30th of May, Corinth was entered by National forces. The 1st Ohio did not participate in the pursuit of the enemy, but remained in and about Corinth, doing picket and guard duty, until the 10th of June when it received marching orders and started for Nashville, passing through Iuka, Tuscumbia, Florence, and Huntsville. At Huntsville, the cars were taken, and the regiment reached Boiling Fork, a tributary of the Elk River on the 7th of July.

On the 14th of July, the regiment went by rail to Tullahoma to repel an anticipated attack on that point, but returned to Cowan Station on the 18th. On the 10th of August, Gen. Joshua W. Sill took command of the brigade and on the 24th the regiment, with its brigade and division, marched for Pelham, where it joined the forces under Gen. Alexander McD. Mcook. On the 28th of August, the regiment marched to Altamont on the Cumberland Mountains and on the 29th and 30th reconnaissances were made down the main road towards Sequatchie Valley. On the afternoon of the 30th, it marched towards Nashville, passing through Manchester, Murfreesboro, and Lavergne, arriving in the vicinity of Nashville on the 7th of September. The march was resumed September 10th at seven P.M., passing through Nashville and across the Cumberland River at three o'clock the next morning.

The regiment had now fairly commenced its march in company with Gen. Buell's army in pursuit of Bragg's Rebel Army, then on its way to Louisville. The race was won by the National forces and Louisville reached on September 26th. It is needless to describe the arduous march or the sufferings of the men on this memorable occasion. The extremely hot weather, the dusty roads, and the almost total absence of drinking water, either for the men or animals, occasioned the most intense suffering and the loss of many valuable lives. But little rest was allowed at Louisville. On October 1st, the march was resumed; the 1st Ohio with its brigade, moving out on the Frankfort Turnpike. Shelbyville was reached on the 2nd and Frankfort on October 6th. This column of troops was under the command of Gen. Joshua W. Sill.

On October 9th, at Dog Walk, a brisk fight was had with the enemy in which the 1st Ohio had a prominent part with the loss of eight or ten men. Lt. Anton Kuhlman (Co. H) was severely wounded. The march was very arduous and at times perilous as it was in the power of the Rebel army to mass and overwhelm the National forces. During most of the time, the enemy hung on the flanks of the National forces and annoyed them in every possible way. A junction with the main army under Gen. Buell was effected on the 11th of

October, two days after the battle of Perryville and the 1st Ohio went into camp on the battlefield.

On the retrograde march through Kentucky, Gen. Buell, commanding the Army of the Ohio, had been superseded by Gen. William S. Rosecrans. Gen. Rosecrans immediately reorganized the whole army; a new name was given it-Army of the Cumberland- and a general change in its structure was made. Gen. Sill, commanding the division in which the first was brigaded, was superseded by Gen. Richard W. Johnson. The name of the corps and division was changed to the 14th Army Corps, Second Division, Right Wing of the Army of the Cumberland.

On December 26, 1862, Gen. Rosecrans having completed his arrangements, the movement on Bragg's army at Murfreesboro commenced. The 1st Ohio moved out on the Nolensville Turnpike with the right wing about noon of the 26th, in the midst of a drenching rainstorm and reached Nolin Creek at four o'clock P.M. During this march almost constant skirmishing was had with Hardee's Rebel corps. This continued to the vicinity of Murfreesboro, which was reached on the 30th, in the midst of the still driving and drenching rain.

On December 31, 1862, the battle of Stones River commenced. The 1st Ohio, at daylight, was stationed on the right with Johnson's Second Division. The pickets were driven in at six o'clock. The 1st Ohio was immediately formed in line of battle and stationed across an open field behind a fence and formed the right of Johnson's front line. Within five minutes, the enemy's skirmishers advanced but were quickly repulsed. Following their skirmishers, the enemy advanced in force but were promptly checked. This action lasted half an hour when another heavy force made its appearance on the right and rear of the 1st Ohio, compelling the regiment to fall back. In effecting this, it encountered the Louisville Legion, which formed the second line, at a time when it was making a change of front to meet the onset on its flank. This created some confusion in both regiments. Order was partially restored, however, and the fight continued, but the entire national right wing was so hardly pressed that it was forced back on the center, creating for a time much confusion. After several ineffectual attempts at a stand, it finally reached the line of Nashville & Chattanooga Railroad. At this point it was reinforced, held the enemy in check, and finally drove them back. After hard fighting, a line was battle was re-established and maintained until the close of the action.

When the 1st Ohio was driven from its line, it was broken into squads, several of which skirmished with the enemy and did good service in checking his onset. One under Lt. Dornbush of Co. B repulsed an attack from the enemy's cavalry. Before reaching the Nashville railroad, the bulk of the regiment was rallied by Major Joab A. Stafford (commanding the regiment) and formed on the right of the 6th Ohio, where it fought gallantly until driven back. During the 1st, 2nd, and 3rd of January, there was considerable maneuvering by the enemy and some skirmishing. On the 2nd of January, a heavy attack was made on the left of the National lines. In this attack, the 1st Ohio did not participate. On January 4th, it was ascertained that the enemy had evacuated Murfreesboro and on the

6th, the 1st Ohio passed through that place and went into camp four miles out on the Shelbyville Turnpike. While lying in Murfreesboro, the army was reorganized and the 1st Ohio was placed in the Second Division of the Twentieth Army Corps.

On June 24, 1863, the movement on Tullahoma commenced. The enemy was encountered on the first day's march at Liberty Gap, 12 miles from Murfreesboro. The 1st Ohio was not actively engaged in this affair, being held in reserve, but was under a heavy artillery fire. On June 26th at 8 P.M., the regiment was withdrawn from the picket line, leaving its fires burning, and made a night march of five miles through rain and deep mud to Millersburg. The march on Tullahoma was one of the most severe the regiment ever experienced, the rain falling constantly and the roads rendered almost impassable from the mud and broken down vehicles. Manchester, Tennessee was reached on June 29th. At this place, all the extra baggage of the army, including the knapsacks of the men, were sent back to Murfreesboro. On July 1st, the regiment passed through Manchester and arrived at Tullahoma at one o'clock at night. At this place, extensive Rebel camps were found- tents still standing-artillery shells lying at the depot. On the 2nd, these shells by accident exploded, killing two members of the 1st Ohio and wounding several others.

On August 16th, the line was march was resumed, passing through Estell Springs, Winchester, Salem, across Smoky Mountain, through White and Paint Rock Gaps, and encamping at Bellefonte on the Memphis & Charleston Railroad on the 22nd. On August 20th, the Chickamauga campaign was initiated and the 1st Ohio moved to Stevenson, Alabama. It crossed the Tennessee at Caperton's Ferry on August 31st. On September 2nd, it ascended the Sand or Raccoon Mountains and marched across them to Winston's Gap. On September 9th, it crossed the Lookout range of mountains- a march of 23 miles.

On the afternoon of the 13th of September, the troops were recalled from Broomtown Valley. They re-crossed the Lookout range, and moving down the valley, again ascended Lookout on the 16th, passing along its crest and descending to Catlett's Gap, near Pond Springs, having marched 26 miles in one day. On September 18th, the 1st Ohio was placed on picket near the right of the National lines. There was constant firing between the pickets during this day. At nine o'clock A.M. of the 18th, the regiment was relieved from picket duty and marched to the support of Gen. Thomas, was placed in line of battle with the Second Division, and directed to recover the ground from which Gen. Baird's division had just been driven with great slaughter. The position of the 1st Ohio was in the front line on the right of the Fourth Brigade. While forming its line and preparing for a charge, it was subjected to heavy firing. Two men were torn from its ranks by round shot.

The charge was made and the enemy driven from the captured position, leaving in our hands all the artillery that had been captured from Terrill in the morning with the addition of two guns belonging to the enemy. The enemy was steadily driven for a mile and a half, and to a point far beyond the ground occupied by Baird in the morning. At this point, the regiment halted and the brigade commanders formed a line of battle which was quickly assailed by the enemy in a determined effort to recover their losses. The attack was handsomely repulsed and two more pieces of artillery captured.

Additional reinforcements were brought up by the enemy and about sunset he was observed massing troops in front for another attack. Before this time, orders had been received by the brigade commanders to fall back to the main National lines, which were not acted upon because of some misunderstanding respecting the picket lines. About dusk, the enemy came up in great force, crushing back the right brigade and seriously shaking the center, the left of which, composed of the 15th Ohio Infantry, fell back in confusion. This compelled the 1st Ohio (which joined the 15th Ohio on the left, at an angle of about 120 degrees), to change its position in order to confront the enemy. In performing this movement, the 1st Ohio was compelled to fall back about 150 yards where it reformed its lines, A most terrific fight ensued in the gathering darkness, added to which the smoke from the discharge made it impossible to see anything in front but the flash of the enemy's guns. A Rebel battery which had been brought close up to the front of the National line lost every horse and every man by the murderous fire poured into it. Such a contest could not last long, and the fight soon ceased, the enemy having fallen back. The division now received orders and fell back to a point where it had left its knapsacks and laid down for the night.

Early on the following morning, rude breastworks were thrown up in front of the National lines; the 1st Ohio occupied the second line of entrenchments. At eight o'clock, the enemy attacked the left of the National lines and extended his attack around the line. The National skirmishers were rapidly driven in, and the enemy appeared in force in front, but unable to withstand the withering fire by which he was received, fell back almost immediately, and could not afterward be brought to close work. About one o'clock P.M., a heavy Rebel force which had passed around the National left wing was observed driving some scattering soldiers through an open woods almost in the immediate rear of the National lines. The 1st Ohio and the Louisville Legion were quickly "about-faced." Advancing to the edge of the timber through which the National lines ran, they delivered a volley and charged. The Rebels instantly gave way and fled. The 1st Ohio was then ordered back to its position in line.

At sunset, orders were received from Gen. Thomas to fall back upon Mission Ridge. The Rebels at this time were swarming over the entrenchments thrown up by Reynolds' command, which had fallen back in obedience to orders. These works were to the immediate right of the position occupied by the 1st Ohio. The broad open field in front of the regiment was crossed under fire but with slight loss. Gen. Steedman and his command were met at this point, having also fallen back. Pausing to form the troops, the National forces marched to Rossville unpursued by the enemy. The loss of the regiment in killed and wounded in this battle was 120, the majority of whom fell in the terrific fight of Saturday evening. Lt. John W. Jackson, a resident of New Lisbon, Ohio, was killed in this action. He was a gallant and meritorious officer and greatly lamented by his fellow soldiers. A gallant soldier, Sgt. Burgdorf, was also killed. Among the wounded were Lt. Dornbush, Lt. Grove, and Lt. Hallenberg. The last named fell into the hands of the enemy.

On September 21st, at daylight, a line of battle was formed and breastworks thrown up. The day was spent awaiting an attack from the enemy, but he did not appear. At half past twelve on the morning of the 22nd, the National forces withdrew and marched into Chattanooga. In forming the lines around the city, the 1st Ohio was placed on the left of the Chattanooga road, its right resting at the bridge over Chattanooga Creek, where it lay for one and a half hours under the fire of two Rebel batteries without being able to return a shot. The loss of the regiment from the cannonading was one killed and five wounded. This position as occupied by the 1st Ohio until the night of the 25th of September, fighting the enemy by day and building the earthworks by night. It then fell back to the second line of works, and for the first time in eight days the men were allowed to throw off their accoutrements and rest in comparative safety, From the beginning of March 1863 up to and including the battle of Chickamauga, Lt. Col. Bassett Langdon was in command of the 1st Ohio.

About the 20th of October, the Twentieth Corps was consolidated with the Fourth Corps and the 1st Ohio was brigaded under General Hazen in the Third Division of that corps. On the 20th of October, the 1st Ohio had formed part of the important expedition down the Tennessee River to Brown's Ferry, which resulted in the surprise and capture of the ridge commanding the ferry, and the roads between Lookout Valley and the Raccoon Mountains, thus enabling supplies to reach Chattanooga. In this affair, Surgeon John C. Barr received a flesh wound in the arm while crossing the river under the fire of the enemy.

On November 23, 1863, the battle of Orchard Knob was fought-really the opening of the battle of Missionary Ridge. About noon of that day, the 1st Ohio, consolidated with the 23rd Kentucky, the whole under the command of Lt. Col. Bassett Langdon, was formed in column doubled on the center to the right of Hazen's brigade. It immediately advanced on the enemy, driving in his pickets and attacking his rifle pits on the knob. The pits and 150 prisoners were captured, and the Rebels driven into their entrenchments at the foot of Mission Ridge. The night was spent in reversing the rifle pits and constructing other defensive works. This position was held until the afternoon of the 25th.

At half past three on the 25th of November, the 1st Ohio was placed in the front line on right of the brigade and division. At the signal of three guns, the forces moved off and were saluted by the enemy's batteries on the crest of the ridge, some 30-40 guns in number. The space to be traversed was about one mile, mostly open ground. The movement was performed in quick time to within 300 yards, when the troops charged on the double-quick, and the Rebels were fairly lifted out of their works almost without firing a shot. The National forces, in obedience to orders, took possession of the abandoned works and sought to protect themselves within them. While occupying this position, the 1st Ohio suffered severely and it became apparent that the only safe course left was to make a dash at the top of the ridge. Lt. Col. Langdon was the first to see the necessity. Getting his regiment in line and rising to the height of the occasion, he pointed with his sword to the summit of the ridge and moved on. The whole command caught the inspiration and mounted the almost perpendicular sides of the hill with an energy superhuman. The enemy was amazed at the audacity of the movement but contested the fight with stubbornness.

The intensity of the Rebel fire was such that five color-bearers of the 1st Ohio were either killed or wounded. The last one, Capt. Trapp of Co. G, was wounded twice within 20 paces of the crest of the hill while gallantly heading the regiment. At this time, the regiment had assumed the shape of a letter A. The nature of the ground being such as to protect the head of the regiment from the Rebel fire in its front, it was halted to gather strength for the final charge. A few minutes sufficed to effect this, and the first and second lines moved up in mass, breaking over and carrying the enemy's works and the crest of the hill. While directing the movement at the head of the column and within about 20 paces of the crest, Lt. Col. Langdon was shot in the face, the ball coming out at the back of the neck. The shock of the ball disabled him for a few minutes, but he recovered his feet and charged with his men to within ten paces of works when the loss of blood forced him to retire, not, however, without witnessing the capture of the Rebel works. Major Stafford of the 1st Ohio was wounded at the foot of the hill, but accompanied his regiment to the top, and carried the flag into the works on the crest. Lt. Christopher Wollenhaupt and Sgt. Major Ogden Wheeler were killed near the crest of the ridge. The entire loss of the regiment was five officers and 78 men killed and wounded.

On November 28, 1863, the 1st Ohio started with other regiments and marched to the relief of Gen. Burnside at Knoxville. On this march and during the East Tennessee campaign, the men suffered intensely from cold, scanty rations, and ragged clothing. On January 17, 1864, the regiment had a brisk engagement with the enemy at Dandridge, losing some men. During this campaign, the 1st Ohio volunteered three different times to re-enlist as veterans, but on each occasion was prevented from doing so by apprehension of attack and other causes. On one of these occasions the men had actually marched six miles on their way homeward.

On May 4, 1864, the 1st Ohio started with Sherman's forces on the Atlanta campaign. On the 10th of May at Buzzard's Roost, it had a skirmish in which Capt. Dornbush and six men were wounded and three killed. On May 14th it had another engagement near Resaca with the loss of two killed and 16 wounded. Among the severely wounded was Capt. Louis Kuhlman of Co. D. The next day it suffered a loss of four killed and 12 wounded. May 17th near Adairsville, a sharp skirmish was had with the enemy. Loss, two killed and two wounded. Among the latter was Lt. George McCracken of Co. H. On May 27th at Burnt Hickory, the regiment lost two officers, Lts. Dickson and Grove, and eight men killed, two officers and 71 men wounded. On June 17th at Kennesaw, eight men were wounded. At the crossing of the Chattahoochee River, two men were killed. After this affair, the regiment did not meet with any notable encounters.

Almost immediately thereafter it commenced to be mustered out by companies- the last one on the 14th of October.

During its term of service, the 1st Ohio was engaged in 24 battles and skirmishes, and had 527 officers and men killed or wounded. It saw its initial battle at Bull Run and closed its career in front of Atlanta. It marched 2,500 miles and was transported by car and steamboat 950 miles.

Subject Index

Anderson, Nicholas (80)
Asbell, Sylvester (69, 81)
Baldwin, Philemon Prindle (99, 103-104)
Barr, Jacob C. (81, 114)
Barrett, John F. (42)
Bennett, James Wesley (81, 91)
Berry, William W. (105)
Bickford, S.B. (120)
Bowers, Henry (111, 116)
Bowles, Thomas (111, 116)
Bowling Green, Kentucky (54)
Boyer, Thomas W. (104)
Braden, Joseph (49, 61)
Brock, George W. (88)
Brown, John F. (31)
Brownlow's Whig and Rebel Ventilator (118)
Butterfield, Benjamin (10, 15, 19, 55)
Buchanan, President James (11)
Bull Run, First Battle of (21-27)
Camden, New Jersey (12-13)
Camp Andy Johnson, Tennessee (53)
Camp Armstrong, Kentucky (36)
Camp Corwin, Ohio (28-33)
Camp McClelland, Pennsylvania (12)
Camp Nevin, Kentucky (37-41)
Camp Sherman, D.C. (15)
Camp Upton, Virginia (18)
Camp Wood, Kentucky (43-52)
Camp Yoke, Kentucky (33)
Carlis, William (52)
Carpenter, Harry W. (73)
Carpenter, Lewis (73)
Carroll, George W. (59, 69)
Carty, W.J. (120)
Chappell, Robert B. (81, 105)
Chattanooga (122-123)
Chickamauga, Battle of (97-107)
Clark, A.L. (122)
Clifford, Jim (89)
Cloud, William (51, 69)
Collier, Jim (40, *41*)
Colwell, James (51, 69)

Connell, Benjamin F. (14)
Copeland, Caleb (52, 107)
Corinth, Mississippi (67-69)
Cormany, George (89)
Cowan Station, Tennessee (70-72)
Crowe, John (33)
Daugherty, Hugh (16)
Davis, Samuel W. (81)
Dayton, Ohio (29)
Dennis, Jeremiah (29)
Denny, Dennis (81)
Dilger, Mathias (111)
Dinsmore, Samuel P. (29)
Dornbush, Henry (79-81, *85,* 100, 104, 106)
Doty, William (91-92)
Duncan, William (36)
Durbin, Frank (48)
Ewing, John (111)
Field, Charles (16)
Foy, James C. (115)
Franklin, Kentucky (54)
Frazer, Christian (84)
Fricker, George (69)
Frizzell, Frederick (69)
Galloway, Henry (36)
Gibson, William Harvey (38, 64, 81)
Giesy, Henry H. (61)
Gordon, James (29)
Grandlienard, Charles E. (84, 87)
Grayson, Lemuel (31)
Gregory, Myron (84)
Griffith, George (69)
Groff, Joseph F. (30, 33, 120)
Grove, George J. (100, 106, 115)
Haason, Jacob K. (59)
Hallenberg, Gustav (100, 106)
Hambright, Henry A. (119)
Harrisburg, Pennsylvania (9-10)
Harvey, William (52)
Hawkins, Joseph (10, 15, 31)
Hayward, George L. (78-80)
Heberly, John (42)
Heberly, William (84, 87)
Heist, Thomas (69)
Hill, James (31)

Homan, Solomon E. (59, 69, 74, 82, 115, 120)
Holtzman, John Reese (52, 55, 69)
Hooker, Emanuel T. (33, 56, 58, 59, 69, 80, 82-83, 89, 104-106, 115)
Hooker, Jared T. (82)
Hughes, John G. (18)
Hunter, Thomas Milton (15, 16, 19, 111)
Huntsville, Alabama (71)
Indian Creek, Alabama (69)
Jackson, Ezra (61)
Jackson, John W. (100, 106)
Johnson, Richard W. (80)
Johnson, William R. (69)
Jones, James E. (115)
Keller, Augustus R. (122)
Kingston, Georgia (119-121)
Kinser, Squire (61)
Kirk, Edward N. (64)
Knoxville, Tennessee (116-119)
Kuhlman, Anton (81)
Kutz, Charley (88, 115, 122)
Lamotte, John (70)
Lamotte, Joshua (88)
Lancaster, Pennsylvania (10)
Langdon, Elisha Bassett (30, 40, 45, 56, 82, 100-107, *108*, 114-115)
Latta, William (91)
Lehman, Jacob (49)
Leonard, George P. (104, 115)
Lewis, Solomon (69)
Linn, Christian "Kitty" (10, 16, 22)
Losh, Andrew (107)
Lydy, Soc (48)
McCarthy, John (106-107)
McCleery, Sam (88, 122)
McCook, Alexander McDowell (16, 18, 19, *20*, 24-27, 28, 31, 32, *35*, 37, 38, 43, 49, 52, 66, 70)
McKinney, George D. (18)
McLaughlin, William W. (111)
Macklin, George (92)
Manler, John H. (29, 69)
Mason, Isaac (52, 69)
Miller, William D. (106, 107)

Missionary Ridge, Battle of (109-116)
Moore, Jacob (69)
Morris, William (58, 59)
Murfreesboro, Tennessee (76-90)
Murphy, David (74)
Myers, George W. (84, 87, 120)
Nashville, Tennessee (54-56)
Negley, James Scott (47)
Neibling, James (48, 70, 89)
Nashville, Tennessee (73-74)
Nichols, Asa (13)
O'Connell, Patrick (80)
Ohio State Fair (30)
Orman, Henry (61)
Orman, Jake (73)
Parrott, Edwin A. (18, 19, 32, 33, *35*, 40, 45, 56, 82)
Parrott, Joseph S. (18, 45)
Patterson, William (106, 115)
Payton, Bailie (52)
Perry, Alvah (73)
Philadelphia, Pennsylvania (12-14)
Pine Hill Camp, Virginia (16)
Pomeroy, George A. (80)
Poulton, Minor R. (33, 92)
Prayson, Lem (48)
Prentice, George D. (34, 47)
Prentiss, Benjamin F. (80)
Pugh, William H. (122)
Reber, Benjamin (29, 69)
Reber, George W. (29)
Reed, John W. "Jack" (30, 55, 81, 86-88, 120)
Rhodes, David (120)
Richards, Dan (48, 70, 89)
Richards, Tom (89)
Ricketts, Ezra (9, 15, 19)
Riddle, William B. (107)
Road, David (29)
Robinson, William F. (18)
Rosecrans, William Starke (*75*)
Rousseau, Lovell Harrison (47, *57*, 58, 61-65)
Saylor, George W. (69)
Schenk, Robert (18, 19, 21, 24-27)

Schopp, Martin (59, 69)
Scott, John C. (31)
Shannon, John A. (29, 80, 92, 106)
Shannon, Robert (13, 30. 120)
Shaw, Dock (48)
Shaw, Homer C. (70-71)
Sherman, William Tecumseh (22, 38-39, 61, 111, 120)
Shetzley, William (59, 69)
Shiloh, Battle of (56-67, 71)
Shook, Jacob (52, 69)
Smith, Benjamin F. (32, 37, 40, 44, 55-57)
Smith, Christopher F. (51, 69)
Smith, James (69)
Snodgrass, Alexander T. (80)
Springer, James H. (107)
Stafford, Joab Arwin (9, 11, 15, 19, 30, 31, 47, 48, 51, 56, 59, 60, 71, 76, 79-82, 84, 92, *98*, 100, 102, 105-106, 111, 114-115, 120)
Starling, Jake (40, *41*)
Stinchcomb, James W. (15)
Stoneburner, Eli (52, 69)
Stones River, Battle of (76-81, 86, 89)
Strentz, John (91)
Stuttzman, Levi (69)
Swigert, William (22)
Taylor, Robert M. (107)
Thornberry, Edward (69)
Timmons, Samuel Pryor (69)
Trapp, Nicholas (80, 104, 106, 111, 114, 120)
Tullahoma, Tennessee (91-93)
Varian, Alexander (81, 115)
Ward, Obediah S. (115)
Washington, D.C. (13-16, 21)
Webb, Nimrod A. (81)
Weeks, Jesse (13, 15)
Weldy, Seth (55)
Wherrett, Charles (36)
White, Abner (122)
Wiley, James M. (31, 51, 56, 69, 74)
Williams, Matilda Ann (84)
Willich, August (38, 43-44, 49, 103-105)
Wills, David Montgomery Davidson (31, 69)

Willison, Riley (29)
Wilson, Albert (81)
Winner, Charles N. (106-107)
Wiseman, John (61)
Wolf, Freeman M. (81, 111, 116)
Wollenhaupt, Christopher (115)
Wyman, Ike (48)
Young, Charles (91, 115)
Zollicoffer, Felix (52)
Federal Units:
9th Illinois Infantry (38)
79th Illinois Infantry (79)
6th Indiana Infantry (47, 58, 63-65, 79-81, 84)
5th Indiana Battery (105)
30th Indiana Infantry (79)
32nd Indiana Infantry (38, 43-44, 46, 52)
37th Indiana Infantry (36, 37, 38)
5th Kentucky Infantry (47, 58, 63, 80, 105, 110)
23rd Kentucky Infantry (114-115)
9th Michigan Infantry (36)
2nd New York Infantry (21, 24-27)
79th New York Infantry (14)
2nd Ohio Infantry {3 months' service}, (10, 14, 16, 19, 21, 24-27)
15th Ohio Infantry (38, 105)
17th Ohio Infantry (39, 55, 60, 73-74, 89, 111)
18th Ohio Infantry (36, 37, 38)
21st Ohio Infantry (70)
41st Ohio Infantry (110)
46th Ohio Infantry (60-61, 111)
49th Ohio Infantry (38)
52nd Ohio Infantry (111)
58th Ohio Infantry (61)
90th Ohio Infantry (73, 77, 89)
93rd Ohio Infantry (80, 84, 95, 103, 105, 110)
105th Ohio Infantry (103)
1st Ohio Cavalry (61)
14th U.S. Colored Troops (123)
16th U.S. Colored Troops (123)
15th U.S. Infantry (58)
16th U.S. Infantry (58)
19th U.S. Infantry (56)

Endnotes

[1] Private Christian Linn of Company A. Linn mustered out with the company on August 3, 1861.

[2] Comer is referring to the largest ocean going steamboat of the Civil War era, the nearly 700-foot long *S.S. Great Eastern* launched in 1858. The ship was also known as the *Leviathan.*

[3] A reference to inventor Richard March Hoe (1812-1886) who designed the rotary printing press, an item of special interest to a former "typo."

[4] Colonel Ephraim Elmer Ellsworth of the 11th New York 'Fire Zouaves,' and a personal friend of President Abraham Lincoln, was killed in a confrontation while removing a Rebel flag from the roof of the Marshall House Inn in Alexandria, Virginia on May 24, 1861.

[5] William "Extra Billy" Smith served as a Congressman and Governor of Virginia prior to the war, and later served as the oldest Confederate general to hold a field command at age 65.

[6] Private William Swigert was captured at Bull Run, was exchanged, and then discharged June 18, 1862 at Fort Columbus, New York.

[7] Colonel Benjamin Franklin Smith (1831-1868) led the regiment until June 2, 1862 when he was reassigned to his former regiment, the 6th U.S. Infantry.

[8] George Dennison Prentice, the caustic editor of the *Louisville Journal,* supported the Know-Nothing party in the 1850s and supported Kentucky's retention in the Union but later took issue with many of the Lincoln administration's policies.

[9] All three men survived, but two were discharged shortly after the incident. Private William Duncan was later discharged to accept a promotion as Captain in the 13th U.S. Colored Troops.

[10] The battle of Rowlett's Station, Kentucky was fought December 17, 1861 and gained national renown for Col. August Willich and his 32nd Indiana.

[11] Private William Cloud died of measles on February 25, 1862 at Woodsonville, Kentucky.

[12] Private James Colwell died of measles January 31, 1862 at Woodsonville, Kentucky.

[13] Colonel James Cameron of the 79th New York and brother of Secretary of War Simon Cameron was killed in action July 21, 1861 at the battle of Bull Run. Confederate forces recovered the body after the battle, and despite pleas from Cameron's family, buried it within their lines. After the Army of the Potomac took control of the region in the spring of 1862, Col. Cameron's grave was found, the body disinterred, and sent for burial in Lewisburg, Pennsylvania.

[14] Gen. William S. Rosecrans recalled the origin of this story as occurring in early 1863 while the Army of the Cumberland was encamped at Murfreesboro. "All of my division commanders then were very popular with their men- McCook, Crittenden, Sheridan, Stanley, Rousseau, and Negley; but most of all was Rousseau. Whenever General Rousseau rode through the camps, whether of his own or other divisions, he was cheered to the skies by the men and would almost invariably make them a happy speech that raised more cheers." One afternoon, a commotion was raised in the camp of the troops of Gen. Jefferson C. Davis' division and Gen. Davis dispatched an aide to discover the cause. "Pretty soon he returned and reported that he couldn't find out what it was all about. The troops were wild over something, and it must be either General Rousseau or a rabbit. Any old soldier who has ever witnessed the commotion in camp occasioned by the discovery of a rabbit will understand the situation and the joke." Rosecrans, William Starke. "Rousseau or a Rabbit", *The United Service, Volume VI: New Series.* Philadelphia: L.R. Hamersly & Co., 1891, pgs. 92-93

[15] Private Benjamin Reber died at Corinth, Mississippi on May 28, 1862.

[16] Private David Murphy died of disease of the heart on November 24, 1862 in Louisville. His brother James Murphy was promoted to Corporal, then Sergeant and died on July 10, 1864 of wounds received the preceding day at the Battle of Chattahoochee Bridge.

[17] Private Nimrod A. Webb died of wounds January 14, 1863 at Nashville, Tennessee.

[18] Comer's note regarding Col. Smith's report of the battle of Shiloh is intriguing as it does not reside in the Official Records of the War of the Rebellion.

[19] An insight into Comer's difficulties with Captain Hooker is found in a letter from a fellow member of Company A known by the pen name "Breech Plate." He wrote the *Ohio Eagle* in February 1863 (after lamenting the Emancipation Proclamation) that "another cause of grievance and humiliation in our company is the fact that for some time past we have had a commander in whom we have no confidence." Noting the promotion of several officers out of the company, Breech Plate remarked that "this leaves us with no one but Hooker, who is self-constituted captain, first, and second lieutenant, orderly sergeant, and all the corporals, but in the estimation of the regiment would make but a very poor private, having neither good sense, sound judgment, or command of his temper or legs. He is, however, an excellent grumbler." *Ohio Eagle,* February 19, 1863, pg. 3

[20] Comer is referencing his continuing struggles with Capt. Emanuel T. Hooker and Sergeant Walter Applegate. Hooker had previously demoted Comer from Second Sergeant to Private in October 1862 citing 'neglect of duty.'

[21] Private John W. (Jack) Reed had been discharged for his wounds on April 30, 1863.

[22] Private James Wesley Bennett of Company A was killed July 2, 1863 at Tullahoma, Tennessee.

[23] Colonel Philemon Prindle Baldwin of the 6th Indiana Infantry led the Third Brigade of Johnson's Division at both Stones River and Chickamauga. He was killed in action on September 19, 1863 at Chickamauga and his remains were never recovered. It is thought that he is buried amongst the unknown dead at Chattanooga National cemetery.

[24] Corporal John Ewing survived his wound and mustered out with Company I on September 14, 1864.

[25] Corporal Thomas Bowles of Company A had been promoted to the rank of Corporal only three days prior to being shot down carrying the regimental colors at Missionary Ridge. He survived the wound, receiving a discharge for disability on June 6, 1864.

[26] Sergeant Freeman M. Wolf of Company A died of his wounds December 5, 1863.

[27] Private Henry Bowers of Company A died in Chattanooga on November 26, 1863 of the effects of his wound.

CPSIA information can be obtained
at www.ICGtesting.com
Printed in the USA
LVHW102128130122
708571LV00027B/726